MAMAN, WHAT ARE WE CALLED NOW?

Persephone Book N° 115
Published by Persephone Books Ltd 2015

First published by Les Éditions de Minuit in 1957
and by Éditions Stock as a Livre de Poche in 2009, with
the title *Ceux qui ne dormaient pas: Journal, 1944–46*

Endpapers taken from a textile designed for
l'Atelier Offner in Lyon 1939–42.

Photographs on pp. 111–119 taken from *Europe's Children
1939–43* (1943) by Thérèse Bonney © The Bancroft Library,
University of California at Berkeley

Typeset in ITC Baskerville by
Keystroke, Wolverhampton

Printed and bound in Germany by
GGP Media GmbH, Poessneck

9781910263051

Persephone Books Ltd
59 Lamb's Conduit Street
London WC1N 3NB
020 7242 9292

www.persephonebooks.co.uk

MAMAN, WHAT ARE
WE CALLED NOW?

by

JACQUELINE MESNIL-AMAR

*translated from the French
(original title* Ceux qui ne dormaient pas:
Journal 1944–46) *by*

FRANCINE YORKE

with a new preface by

CAROLINE MOOREHEAD

and with photographs by

THÉRÈSE BONNEY

PERSEPHONE BOOKS
LONDON

PREFACE

On 18th July 1944 Jacqueline Mesnil-Amar began to keep a diary. She had written many things in the past – articles and reviews for magazines, jottings of every kind in notebooks, often working late at night – but this was something different. In the last frenzied weeks of the German occupation of Paris her husband André had disappeared. She wanted to record her thoughts, her fears, her desperate hopes, her memories, along with a description of Paris itself, as the German soldiers pulled out and de Gaulle's Free French arrived. When she abandoned her diary, five weeks later, Paris was free and André, miraculously, was alive.

The Amars were both Jewish, from families who saw themselves as totally assimilated, French first and Jewish second. André was descended from a Sephardic banking family from Salonika which had settled in Paris in 1919. He had attended the prestigious Lycée Condorcet, and afterwards taken a degree in philosophy at the École Normale Supérieure, before joining his father's bank. In 1930, at the age of 22, he married 21-year-old Jacqueline, the daughter of Jules Perquel, a financier and the editor of a paper called *Le Capital*. The

Perquels were an old Jewish family from Lorraine. Ellen Allatini, Jacqueline's mother, was Italian, and came from Florence, but was brought up in Salonika. While Jacqueline was growing up, they lived in the smart suburb of Passy, and she would later write a somewhat mordant account of what it had been like as a small child to be a part of the high French bourgeoisie in this 'cradle of Parisian Jewry', where every man pursued the same career in banking, finance or the civil service, and everyone ate at the same restaurants, played golf or rode at weekends, took their holidays on the Nile, kept English cars and read, providing they were intellectual enough, Proust and the Goncourt brothers. With her two sisters, Jacqueline and the nanny took walks in the surroundings woods.

Jacqueline, like André, was clever. She spoke Italian and English, had taken a degree in literature and planned to write a thesis on poetry and Catholicism. Both were passionate about French culture and the arts, and in their flat in central Paris the young couple invited friends to talk late into the night about what they were reading and seeing and thinking. Under the pen name Delphine, Jacqueline contributed articles to magazines, light-hearted sketches of society life, and theatre reviews. She had a natural talent for story-telling, and an easy, agreeable style. With André's younger brother Emmanuel, she wrote a synopsis for a ballet to be called *Night Dragonfly*, and she started a novel. In the evenings, bored with the world of bankers, André continued with his philosophy studies. In 1934, they had a daughter, Sylvie. No more than a couple of times a year did they attend a synagogue or celebrate a Jewish holiday. Religion was of no great consequence

to either one of them, as it was not to the great majority of assimilated French Jews in the early 20th century. More observant were the foreign Jews, those who, fleeing persecution in Germany and Eastern Europe in the 1930s, had sought and been given refuge in France during the welcoming years of the left-wing Blum government. Of the 330,000 Jews said to be living in France just before the war, around half were foreign, without French nationality – a distinction that would soon come to matter a great deal.

When the war broke out, André became a lieutenant in the French army and left for the front along the Maginot line, the great wall of cement fortifications built to withstand a German invasion. Jacqueline and Sylvie were in Paris when, in a matter of hours, the Germans broke through, advanced and entered the city on 14th June 1940. Together with many other Parisians, they were part of the *exode*, the flight southwards in a river of cars, hay wagons, furniture vans, ice-cream carts, hearses and horse-drawn drays, dragging behind them wheelbarrows and prams, described by Jacqueline as 'like a burning Pompeii, fleeing the German lava'. They were fortunate in having a car and, taking Marie the nanny with them, were able to reach Bordeaux.

When André was demobilised – he was one of the more fortunate, for some 1.8 million French soldiers were captured and sent to labour and prison camps in Germany – they settled in Aix-les-Bains, in one of the provinces occupied by the Italians, who treated those they had conquered with rather greater humanity than the Nazis. As part of the armistice signed between Maréchal Pétain and the Germans, the geography of France had been redrawn. Apart from the area

occupied by the Italians in the south-east, 49 of France's 87 mainland departments – three-fifths of the country – were now occupied by Germany, which was to control the Atlantic and the Channel coasts and have the right to large portions of French raw materials. Below a heavily guarded demarcation line, cutting France in half, lay Vichy France, in theory a legal, sovereign state ruled over by Pétain. The 83-year-old hero of Verdun was already somewhat frail.

From Aix-les-Bains the Amars followed, with growing horror, the first *Statut des Juifs*, with its definition of who, exactly, counted as Jewish, and its exclusion of Jews from a wide number of professions; the way that Vichy, going ahead of German demands and calling for a 'full-scale purification of Jews' was busy confiscating – stealing – Jewish property; the order, in May 1942, that all Jews over the age of six in the German zone should wear a yellow star. And, soon, they heard about the *rafles*, the terrifying manhunts and round-ups of Jews, and their deportation, on cattle trucks, to unknown destinations in the east. It was very hard to believe that the first country to emancipate and integrate its Jews as full citizens, during the 1789 revolution, had turned so rapidly and so readily against them. Harder still, soon after, to learn that the Germans had been amazed by the alacrity with which the French responded to their offers of rewards for anyone who denounced a Jew. Later, it would be calculated that three and a half million denunciations had been handed in, many signed by *un bon Français*, or a 'little woman who only seeks to do her duty', though many of these, of course, were from covetous neighbours or to report black marketeers.

André's parents and elderly grandmother were all in Aix-
les-Bains, as was Emmanuel, his wife Suzie and their young
child. They were safe, for the moment, though there was not
much to eat and Marie queued endlessly for milk for the baby.

In 1942, during a visit to Marseille, André made friends
with a group of young Zionists, and helped them to start a
paper they called *Chem*. He also joined the *Organisation Juive
de Combat*, a resistance network which had started life in
Warsaw and consisted mainly of foreign Jews.

On 11th November 1942, the Germans, having carefully
laid their plans, swept down through the whole country,
occupying not only Vichy France, but the Italian zone as well.
Until this moment, Jews hiding in these two areas had been
relatively secure, particularly if they had French nationality.
The round-ups in the occupied north had already taken large
numbers of Jews to Drancy, a holding camp on the outskirts
of Paris, and from there to Auschwitz, along with many foreign
Jews obligingly handed over to the Nazis by the Vichy government. From this moment on, no one would be safe; the
promises made by Pétain to safeguard the French Jews at
the expense of the foreign ones, would be shown to be worth-
less. The *rafles* intensified; train after train left Drancy for
Auschwitz.

It was not long before Emmanuel was caught and
deported. Suzie was arrested and sent to a prison in Turin.
André's parents and his grandmother tried to escape to
Switzerland but, waiting in a hotel on the border, they were
denounced by one of its employees. They, too, were now sent
to Drancy. André, Jacqueline and Sylvie, provided with false

identity cards and new names, followed them to Paris, hoping to find some way to secure their release. They failed to do so. In October 1943, the Amar parents and grandmother were put on a train to the Nazi camps.

André rented a flat, under their false names, at 6 Rue de Seine. Here he wrote and roneoed tracts and clandestine leaflets and gave refuge to other *résistants*. Sylvie was sent to a private school, where her aunt, Jacqueline's sister, was teaching. M Perquel was being hidden by the family cook; Mme Perquel, whose Italian nationality continued to give her a little protection, stayed on in the family apartment, though repeatedly visited and threatened by the Nazis. On one occasion, she would have been arrested had it not been for the quick-witted concierge who was able to warn her in time for her to hide in the attics.

Paris was grey and very cold. Coupons were needed for bread, soap, school supplies, meat and much else besides. Parisians were advised not to eat the rats which had emerged, starving, from the sewers, 'enormous, long-whiskered, dark-coated, red-eyed'. The word 'ersatz' had entered everyday vocabulary, with housewives exchanging tips on how to crush grape pips for oil, and roll cigarettes from a mixture of scarce tobacco, Jerusalem artichokes, sunflowers and maize, as they queued interminably for ever-dwindling amounts of food. With supplies of linen, wool, cotton, leather and fuel all dried up, Paris clattered to the sound of wooden clogs and horse-drawn carts. Vegetables had been planted in window boxes and in the Tuileries. A relationship between occupier and occupied, complicated, seductive, dangerous, ensnared them

all. What the French would call *le temps des autruches*, the time of ostriches, was in place. Jacqueline Amar's diary provides a remarkable portrait of what it was like to be Jewish during the grey and terrible years of occupation, with danger creeping ever nearer.

With the landings in Normandy on 6th June 1944, and the advance of the Allies towards Paris, resistance work became increasingly perilous. On 18th July, André, who was acting as liaison officer with London, was instructed to meet a British parachutist at the Rue Erlanger. It was a trap. The Gestapo were waiting for him. He was taken to their headquarters in the Rue des Saussaies and tortured, before being put on to a train for Auschwitz, together with fifty other hostages. It was the last deportation train. The date was 17th August 1944.

Against all odds, André came home. Urging his companions to join him, he escaped from the train taking him towards the east and walked 50 kilometres back to Paris. He had been gone 37 days. Hearing that he was alive, Jacqueline wrote, 'there are moments when our lives seem to have been touched by the hand of God'. She, André, Sylvie and her parents had survived. As had Suzie, released from her prison in Turin. But André's parents and grandmother were dead and of Emmanuel there was no news. When the few surviving Jewish deportees started coming home, after the liberation of the camps in the spring of 1945, André and Jacqueline went every day to the Hotel Lutétia, the just-vacated former headquarters of the Abwehr, the Wehrmacht's intelligence service, now turned into a reception centre, hoping that Emmanuel might be among them. They were daunted from

asking too much by the haggard, other-worldliness of the skeletal figures stumbling into the Lutétia. Thirty-one-year-old Emmanuel never came back. He had not even seen his second child, born after his arrest.

Paris, all through the autumn and winter of 1944 and long into 1945 was cold and wretched. The Germans, who had spent the years of occupation in an orgy of looting, had left behind them blasted bridges and bombed railway lines, and then taken away with them coal stocks, railway equipment and trucks. This time, wrote the diarist Jean Galtier-Boissière, it was *la grande fuite des Fritz*. Gas was heavily rationed. The black market, on which so many Parisians had come to depend, had disappeared, and substitute arrangements were plagued by robberies and hijackings. Parisians lived on vegetables, mainly turnips and carrots. They had been reduced, as Janet Flanner wrote in her diary, 'to the primitive problems of survival, of finding something to eat, of hatred, of revenge, of fawning . . . of hiding, like savages'.

More important, as the French took stock of the years of occupation and collaboration, there was the question of blame. It was later said that as the Germans pulled out, some 110,000 French people, fearful of what liberation might bring, requested to go with them – to which the Germans, chillingly, replied: 'We no longer need you.' And 20,000 French women, accused of relations with the enemy, had their heads shaved in the first violent weeks of freedom, when scapegoats were needed to expunge, in purifying rituals, the shameful deeds of occupation. Collaborators were hunted down, shot, sometimes tortured. Trying to restore order, de Gaulle announced that

harsh penalties would be handed down to those convicted of collaboration, and prosecutors and courts worked feverishly to hear the cases of the men and women who had helped the Germans during what soon became known as *les années noires*, the black years.

But then, early in 1945, de Gaulle made a speech. 'The days of weeping,' he said, 'are over. The days of glory have returned.' To restore France to its former position as a great power, the French now had to look forward, not back, to unite in a shared vision of 'the battling France, the only France, the true France, the eternal France.' Conveniently downgrading the role played by the allies in the liberation of France, he declared that the moment to celebrate the *résistants* who had freed France had come, and that all dwelling on collaboration should cease – thereby establishing the myths that would define the years of German occupation for the next quarter century. It was time, he told the French, to move on.

* * *

But it would not be easy. Not for the French, who now struggled to navigate between shame and defiance, though they were much helped by the praise heaped upon the *déportés politiques*, men and women arrested and deported for resistance activities, and by the wilful amnesia which seemed to settle so quickly over much of France. And certainly not for the Jews, neither those who now crept out of hiding and were faced by the devastation of their lives, nor the few who came home from the extermination camps – of the 75,700 deported

fewer than 2000 came home – their mental and physical health often ruined beyond repair, to find their families fractured and few people willing, in the new triumphalist mood of France, to listen to their stories. Nor were they helped by the spirit of what later would be called *résistancialisme*, the idea that France had been a country of *résistants*, not collaborators, and the feeling that to have been deported as a *résistant* was noble, but to have fallen into German hands as a victim was shameful. Even the dead, guilty of passivity, were not immune from this shame, for they had allowed themselves to be corralled by the anti-semitic laws. Simone Veil, the Jewish lawyer and politician who had been deported to Auschwitz, spoke of this as a second death, that of being forgotten. In the organisations founded to celebrate and care for survivors, there was much ambiguity over who had or had not 'conformed to French honour'. *Résistants* were entitled to compensation; the deported Jews were conceded it. It would be many painful years before these attitudes were questioned.

Three weeks after Paris was liberated, André and Jacqueline helped set up an information network for the deported Jews, *Le Service Central des Déportés Israélites*. Jacqueline became the editor of its monthly bulletin, drawing in reports from Switzerland, Poland and Belgium and, after people began coming home from the camps, trying to piece together what exactly had happened and to reunite families scattered by the war. She was also asked to write commentaries for newsreels on the war years.

For André and Jacqueline, it was not easy either. They, too, needed to come to terms with losing relations and friends.

More than that, they had to confront, each in their own way, what having been Jewish and French in the years of occupation said about their own Jewishness. Both emerged profoundly changed.

André returned to his bank but was delighted when, not long afterwards, he was asked to put together a History of Ideas course at the Institut d'Études Politiques in Paris. He threw himself into the work, began teaching Nietsche and Spengler, and was much loved by his students, who accompanied him home in the evenings to recreate something of the intellectual salon of the pre-war years.

Jacqueline, for her part, began to explore in her articles for the monthly bulletin and elsewhere – a number of which form the second part of this book – questions not just about what had happened to the Jews of Europe, but the attitudes and assumptions of European Jews in the years leading up to the war. She wrote about the Warsaw ghetto, Treblinka, Birkenau, and she agonised over whether or not the 'civilised world' had a conscience at all, and how long it would take survivors to find 'themselves' again. She referred to the Holocaust years as 'the long voyage of terror'.

Looking back over her life, she felt a mixture of regret and contempt for the way that the Jewish families she had grown up among had believed so passionately in their own assimilation, had been so willing to adopt the customs and ape the behaviour of the Catholic and Protestant French, and had thus failed to see how profound the differences were between them, 'by reason of suffering and blood'. They had felt so 'good and so safe' in this 'golden age', even after the advent

of Hitler, 'so deaf and so blind to the cries of the persecuted', that they had become the 'Jews of forgetfulness'. Her articles were full of rhetorical questions. Was there any meaning in suffering? Had silence not been indifference, or, worse, complicity? The assimilated Jews had abandoned their ancient values, but their Frenchness had not saved them – were they not now condemned to emptiness? The light-hearted Delphine of the pre-war years had been replaced by a more serious, sadder figure. She now called herself Mesnil-Amar, Mesnil having been the name of a property outside Paris owned by her father before the war. Sylvie, who was ten when the war ended, longed for her mother to return to the fabulous stories she had once invented and recounted to her with such sparkle.

Instead, what Jacqueline now did was to become involved in the fate of the refugees, thinking of them as thousands of lost souls, calling out to each other 'through the nights of this desolate Europe'. In 1945 there were some 20 million people floating around liberated Europe: prisoners of war, former camp inmates, forced labourers, those unable to go home by virtue of the fact that borders had changed and they no longer had homes to go back to. The Allies managed, despite formidable logistical problems, to return home five million of them by the late summer, but many of the others became embroiled in the politics of resettlement, pawns in the need for immigrant labour in the countries devastated by the war, or rejected as too damaged by what had taken place. In France, demographic experts were recruited to advise on those racial and ethnic characteristics most likely to prove

adaptable. Jacqueline's articles were full of anger. She was furious that so many people had been able to sleep at night and chosen not to listen, not to understand: 'knowing is like love,' she wrote, 'it has to become a passion, or otherwise it means nothing.' She railed against the leniency of the war trials, against the failure of ordinary Germans to have prevented the atrocities happening, just as she railed against the French for accepting Vichy's persecutions and for handing the Jews over to the Nazis.

But nothing made her angrier than the fate of Europe's children. The war had left behind it a continent of orphans and homeless children: some 50,000 in Czechoslovakia, 280,000 in Yugoslavia, 50,000 in Germany. Many had forgotten who they were or where they came from. In the summer of 1945 posters had started appearing on the walls of train stations and post offices across Europe. Put there by the Red Cross, they showed pictures of babies and small children with underneath the words: 'Who am I?' Malnourished, wary, sickly, described by one aid worker as 'tired, wan, broken little old men and women', these children became for Jacqueline the symbol of European culture and humanity in disarray.

In France, as the war ended, the OSE, *L'Organisation de Secours aux Enfants*, founded in Russia on the eve of WW1 to help destitute Jews, and which had played an important part in saving Jewish children in France during the occupation, estimated that there were between five and six thousand Jewish children who were now orphans, whether hidden in non-Jewish homes around the country or over the border in Switzerland or Spain. They needed to be traced, restored

to their proper names and identities and a future found for them. Many of them the children of the Polish and German tailors, knitters, miners and tinkers who had arrived in France in the 1920s and 1930s, their short lives had been marked by exile, camps, loss of parents, clandestinity. They had to be taught how to live with the past, to remember and to redis-cover their childhoods, and they had to be helped to come to terms with feelings of hatred, revenge and humiliation. How, asked Jacqueline in her articles, can you ever make these children 'normal'? How give them the childhood they never had? How stop them regarding adults as enemies, for adults had crushed their parents? It was 'not an act of charity but one of justice' and a 'duty', she wrote, to care for them, in such a way that they would 'once again belong to the human family'. 'We must give them hope, for they represent our only hope for a world in which we have failed.'

As time passed, both André and Jacqueline became ever more immersed in Judaism until, as Sylvie later wrote, it 'devoured' their thinking. Some of their friends, finding their concerns obsessive, became estranged, and even Sylvie protested that they thought about little else. In André it took the form of a diminishing interest in philosophy, saying that there was nothing of any merit when it lacked an ethical dimension. Studying and reading incessantly, he learnt Hebrew and sought morality in the laws conveyed to Moses on Mount Sinai. Increasingly, he felt no tolerance towards critics of the state of Israel. In his 60s, on one of their now frequent visits to Israel, he had the bar mitzvah he had never had as a boy.

Jacqueline, no less immersed, followed a somewhat different trajectory. She felt herself to be profoundly rooted in Europe, and would say that her spiritual life had been marked by three cities, the Florence of her mother's family, Jerusalem and Paris. She embarked on a series of studies and talks on the Jewish characters to be found in Proust, Anatole France, Zola and Balzac, and these became widely praised articles in various magazines.

In 1957, she decided to publish her war diary, along with some of the articles written immediately after the war, under the title *Ceux qui ne dormaient pas*. But it was too soon. France was still amnesiac about its war, not ready for such raw and accusatory material. It was not in fact until May 1968, when the young began to question everything, and 1971 when Marcel Ophuls's film *Le Chagrin et la Pitié* – 280 unflinching minutes of life in Clermont-Ferrand under the occupation – was released, and 1973 with the French edition of Robert Paxton's *Vichy France: Old Guard and New Order*, that the French at last began to face up to their *années noires*. Jacqueline, who died in 1987, lived long enough to witness a complete reappraisal of Vichy and the occupiers, but she was not alive when some of the most culpable collaborators – Klaus Barbie, René Bousquet, Maurice Papon – were finally brought to trial in the late 1980s and 1990s. Nor did she live to see the success of *Ceux qui ne dormaient pas* when it was reissued in France in 2009 (and was then translated into Spanish and Italian).

Jacqueline spent the last years of her life reading. Always frail, she also suffered from depression, but her immense

pleasure in literature never deserted her. She read and reread the classics she had loved from a very young age: Shakespeare, Proust, the tragedies of Racine. When she died, Sylvie put in her coffin Chateaubriand's *L'Itinéraire de Paris à Jerusalem*. It seemed to her the perfect companion for a woman who had devoted so much thought to her own journey into the past.

Caroline Moorehead

London, 2015

MAMAN, WHAT ARE
WE CALLED NOW?

PART I
DIARY OF A TRAGIC TIME

PART I
DIARY OF A TRAGIC TIME

18TH JULY 1944 RUE DE SEINE 11 PM

André[1] hasn't come back tonight.

25TH JULY

A week has gone by since then. I lay on my bed, fully dressed and wide awake; Marie, who hasn't left me for an instant, was asleep beside me, sighing deeply, her large bosom rising and falling with each breath.

I was straining to hear the slightest sound, longing for the familiar rapid footsteps outside the door, but they never came. A thousand times I thought I'd heard one of the sounds that are so much a part of the man I love – the jangle of his keys, the click of the door handle, his little smoker's cough, the rustle of a newspaper – and the sound of his cheerful voice

1   André Amar (1908–90) married Jacqueline Mesnil-Amar in 1930. His family was from Salonika, his father Saül Amar was a banker. André was a graduate teacher of philosophy. He was head of the Parisian section of the Jewish Resistance network OJC (*Organisation Juive de Combat*) (cf. fn.7).

3

calling out his pet name for me from the other end of the flat. But nothing. Complete silence. Always the same all-enveloping silence we endured after the others were arrested.

That evening my younger sister Jo,[2] her fiancé, and our friend Madeleine had come to dinner; I remember the menu – some little treats painstakingly assembled to celebrate their engagement. And we waited . . . I don't know why, but that evening I began to feel afraid from 6 o'clock onwards. A wave of anxiety swept over me. I went into the kitchen to ask Marie to make me some tea; it was warm in there but I was cold as ice and shivering all over.

Marie has been with us for so long I couldn't help dropping the occasional hint about some of the meetings A has been having, and about what our friends have been doing. 'I thought as much! I knew something was going on,' she said over and over again.

By 8 o'clock I was panicking, for no real reason since André is always late. 'What are you worried about? He's stopped off for a drink. He's just late. He ran into some friends,' our guests kept saying, although with less and less conviction. For the sake of my daughter[3] I forced myself to make conversation over dinner, toyed with the roast veal, made a great effort, smiled; but all the time I was more and more anxious. Finally I couldn't bear it any longer. I began to

2   Josette Perquel, studying English at the Sorbonne, a contemporary and friend of Hélène Berr (1921–45), who mentions her several times in her *Journal*, and cf. fn. 79.
3   Sylvie Amar was born in 1934.

do some of the stupid things one does to take one's mind off waiting. A dozen times I walked to the Quai Voltaire and back holding Sylvie's little hand. Her small face was pale, her eyes dark – she understood. It's the waiting that's the worst. Time is the enemy. You struggle with it, trying to conjure up something out of the passing minutes: a figure in the distance, at the end of the street, a familiar outline, desperate to perform a miracle by sheer will-power, to make someone appear on a bicycle, someone who isn't coming, who, you know perfectly well, isn't going to come.

By four in the morning I had telephoned Nadine[4] a dozen times. César[5] wasn't back either. She knew that eight of our men had arranged to meet in the Rue Erlanger at five o'clock that afternoon. We had to face the facts.

And so we took the usual precautions yet again. We left our hiding place in the Rue de Seine, the ninth since the beginning of the war, in a hurry, just as we had left all the previous ones (several members of the group had visited us there). I sent Sylvie on ahead as usual; she had cried so much during the night, that when she woke in the early morning I had to tell her that her *papa* had gone off to the Maquis,[6] and that I'd already had news of him. Yet again I had just

4   Nadine Destouches, or Dessouches, a pianist, girlfriend of César Chamay.
5   César Chamay, an old friend of the Amars, hero of the Jewish resistance, had been deported previously in December 1943. Having escaped, he became Head of Intelligence for the OJC and played an active part with the Paris 'irregulars'. He would be deported from Drancy on 17th August.
6   Rural guerilla bands of resistance fighters called *maquisards*.

a night to dispose of everything connected with the OJC[7] before daylight, lists, carbon copies, letters; I gave it all to Madeleine. She took away the whole incriminating bundle in a hat box.

Since then I've been dashing about all over the place, getting nowhere. I approach all the 'right' people, 'important' people, although they themselves are already beginning to worry that they aren't important any more; I have meetings with people with 'contacts', the ex-mistress of a colonel in the Gestapo (busy painting her toe-nails when I arrived), a former minister in the Vichy government, who was abstracted and interested only in his own safety, the lawyers working for the Germans who adopt the icy tone and the bored look of men who hear the same story a hundred times a day, who reply condescendingly that 'no one is shot straightaway', that is unless they are armed (dear God, how many of them were carrying guns?), that military tribunals are handing out very few sentences at the moment, that judges can sometimes be bribed, and that it's all a question of finding the right intermediary, etc.

Everything just adds to the confusion and the horror, it's all black and shadowy. I'm coming up against a brick wall everywhere. I will sell my rings, I will sell my soul, I will sell my life, but I can't believe even that would be enough. And so I wait, I wait in their rooms, in the offices of men who are

7   OJC *Organisation Juive de Combat*, originally the *Armée Juive*, calling itself the *Mouvement des Jeunesses Sionistes*, Young Zionist Movement, later officially registered as OJC under the French Forces of the Interior, FFI.

seeing 'someone else', lawyers who have been seeing 'someone else' for the last four years, in their luxurious offices – all the more luxurious because of the lucrative caseload resulting from those years. I am living in a nightmare, drowning, sick with worry, struggling with unknown monsters, with exhaustion, anxiety and with death...

For me, the streets are empty, my heart is empty, everything is empty, sometimes even my friends' faces seem empty.

26TH JULY 1944

I went to see Maurice B[8] yesterday, in the hope that his friendly demeanour might be comforting, and to try and find out what he knows about the whole affair. But he seemed tired and depressed, worn out and ... too quiet. He hardly said a word. What does he really know, and, more importantly, what does he really think? His kindness did not make me any less worried. There were three others there, from the same organisation, all talking at once... It seems that there were three or four or possibly five groups and, according to them, our people had recently become reckless to the point of insanity, dragging them all into something from which they are unable to extricate themselves and which could have terrible consequences. Words ... words ... words. T, our young informant, a very elegant young woman, looks utterly drawn

---

8 Maurice Brenner (1907–63), member of the *Armée Juive* since 1942, and of the Paris section since early 1944, responsible (among many other resistance activities) for providing forged papers.

and washed out. Apparently some Spaniards and some English Intelligence Service operatives, who may or may not have been genuine, were rounded up with the others. They also say the reason there was a big raid in the Rue Erlanger, where they used to meet, was because some Germans had been attacked there. Apparently this, apparently that...

I'm worn out by it all, even by the heroism. I stand at the studio window which overlooks the Parc Montsouris, and listen to the birds roosting in the huge trees. It's such a peaceful time of day, yet it would seem perfectly normal if fate decreed that a German car should appear out of nowhere and draw up outside. I keep thinking... last night, in the pitch dark, just before the dawn, I thought you might not... be ... and I faced up to my agony, I shrieked, I cried out, goodness knows what, while I tried to think things through. What I want to know is whether all this is for the Jews or is it for France? Or is that one and the same thing? Or is it above all for freedom? What's it all for? And suddenly I don't understand anything. Everything I valued has turned to dust, I feel as if I have been torn in half and swallowed up in some dark night. And in the end is nothing worth more than the life of someone one loves? Do I no longer believe in anything?

Now the siren has sounded. I walked back from Maurice's, from the University to Madame F's in the Rue de Berne, where my mother and Jo have been hiding for the past four months. For three hours I walked, along the Boulevard Raspail, the Rue de Rennes, to Saint Germain des Prés, and then along the Seine. Through a haze of exhaustion the dome of the Opéra in the distance seemed to be shimmering under

a kind of greenish halo. This endless walk took me through every part of Paris, so many different cities, each one a part of me, my avenues, my streets, the loveliest and the ugliest, the oldest and the newest, and I walked with my eyes half-closed, all of a sudden a stranger in my own city, separated from it by my grief and yet forever bound to it.

27TH JULY 1944

I spent the afternoon lying down, in my little bedroom at Mme P's in the Rue de Clichy. Mme P, whom they call Nana, has taken me in. She runs a little shop selling oil and soap. (My beloved older sister has been in hiding there for over a year with her husband, since he came out of prison.) Mme P squeezed me in, as she has so many others. There is a shaft of sunlight on the angle of the roof beside my window, where the cat is sleeping.

What a woman Nana is! Fierce, loud-mouthed, and yet a princess – holding court in the shop wearing a white overall, or in the kitchen with a blue apron tied round her, just like the old days when she was a concierge sitting in her *loge* in her black dress. Whatever she is doing, whether she's ironing the week's laundry, or welcoming visitors, in her heart, in her principles and in her beliefs she remains a princess. No call for help ever goes unanswered. Since 1940, she has been there tirelessly for everyone, prisoners, escapees, Jewish children, members of the Resistance. And when asked why she takes on so much on top of her everyday work, and why Jewish children, she replies, simply, 'I do it for my country!' Nowadays we are not used to that kind of language.

I am on my narrow iron bed, in the smallest bedroom in the house, and Riki, the cat, has just jumped onto the eiderdown and sent up a cloud of feathers.

Dear God, do people get used to living with this kind of terror?

28TH JULY 1944

Something terrible has happened to my cousin Paule,[9] the group's doctor. It's a complicated story and a miracle that she wasn't taken by the Gestapo's Corsican spies who were surrounding a building she was visiting in order to treat some injured people from the network. A young boy bicycling past was arrested for waving to her. By sheer audacity she managed to escape: I've no idea what story she concocted on the spur of the moment. She hasn't been seen since and is on the run, hiding, establishing a new clandestine life; that's what I've been told. We managed to talk on the telephone but, in spite of her cool-headedness, it's clearly been an awful shock. Apparently the Corsican spies were working for Bonny-Lafont[10]. . . This couldn't be worse. (Anatole de Monzie[11] told me all this yesterday when I went to his flat.) And there's more.

---

9 Doctor Paule Bolvin, who joined the OJC in December 1943, cared for injured members of the Paris Section.

10 The Bonny-Lafont gang: Pierre Bonny (1895–1944) and Henri Lafont (1902–44) ran the French Gestapo from 1940–44.

11 Anatole de Monzie, a lawyer by profession, originally a member of the Republican Socialist party, held several important ministerial posts between 1913 and 1940.

T, our very own 'in-house' conspirator, with her silk turban, earrings and cigarette holder (who is, incidentally, extremely brave), took more than an hour to tell us the whole story, yesterday, when we met in the Café de la Paix. Apparently the German police took Ernest back to his flat – I believe he's one of the most active in the network – and forced him to answer all his phone-calls. Some of his friends rang and heard his voice. It's dreadful. Who gave them away? I am afraid.

That's not all: two French policemen in plain clothes went to see César's concierge. They arrived at Rue de la Tour asking for César and André, using their real names. They searched their rooms, turned everything upside down, and then one of them asked the poor woman, 'Didn't you know that you had *terrorists* here?'

(. . . Dear God, were they armed? And were there any weapons at Ernest's flat?)

Nadine and I had lunch in a restaurant together. We were both dropping with exhaustion, worn out by all the cycling around, all the meetings in cafés, tired of all the snatches of information, garbled messages, more frightful news. The restaurant was in the Rue Boissy-d'Anglas, doubtless packed with Fifth Columnists. But what the hell. We had a good lunch and drank lots of red wine. Meanwhile, they probably won't have eaten a thing for ten days, apart from frightful thin grey prison broth: they'd be lucky even to get that. Nadine told me about her life, sad and quite lonely; lots of parental dramas when she was a child; then a struggle to make a living (she's a musician); a rather gloomy life, with a few bright moments of hope, followed by long periods of disappointment and

waiting, an unfulfilled life, like all lives! And then she met César, our old friend, and found love, only for that to be threatened almost at once. She's got beautiful eyes, rather gentle, dark blue and slightly wary, a small anxious face, and short fluffy hair like duck down. There's something secretive and tense about her, like a small nocturnal animal who's afraid of the light. I didn't tell her about my life.

28TH JULY, LATE EVENING

Every evening Nana comes up from her oil and soap shop (ersatz soap and very little oil) before the radio broadcast begins, which isn't until 11 pm now. We spend the long summer evenings, which are so beautiful and so sad, looking out of the window on to the Rue de Clichy. It's a very busy street where everyone comes and goes like in the opening scene of *Carmen*: all human life is there, day and night.

Jean, my brother-in-law, and Edmond, Nana's husband, take a keen interest in what the three or four tarts in the area get up to. They try to pick up the German soldiers guarding the lorries parked there under their green camouflage, to take them to their lodgings, a vile dump with an entrance hall to make your heart sink. There's one woman, who's 55 at least, who 'had' a colonel the whole of last winter; she's a hideous wreck who wears an old beige hat and a sweater over a printed dress, which clings to her thin body and emphasises the rolls of her flabby stomach. Yet people round here say that her awful fake-crocodile handbag is stuffed with banknotes. And there's another, a fat woman with huge calves who wears a

short-skirted suit, who seems to do quite well: she sometimes goes into the building followed by a succession of hesitant and very young soldiers. Then there's a girl in a flowery hat, wearing lots of cheap rouge, who shouts a lot; she talks the most. They are all heavily made up. Actually, these women lead rather quiet lives; they never leave the *quartier*, so they're not bothered by restrictions on the métro. They have their routine, and they eat on the black market. We think they look anxious but perhaps that's our imagination. . .

This evening there was a brawl and a lot of yelling at 'these twenty-year-old kids who come muscling in on our patch'. I think it was because of a girl from Alsace who is tall and beautiful and wears a pretty floral skirt and a short-sleeved white blouse over her firm breasts. From time to time she turns up looking irresistible and wreaks havoc. Nana tells us these women come into her shop and buy sweets for all the street kids in the Rue de Clichy. What the men say about them doesn't bear repeating.

29TH JULY

A crazy day, one false trail after another. My friend Raymonde thinks it's all to do with forged documents: according to her, our men were taken first to the French police headquarters and from there to the Santé[12] for being in possession of forged

---

12 La Santé was one of the most famous prisons in France. Situated in the XIVe arrondissement of Paris, it was used during the Occupation to house Resistance fighters and Communists as well as ordinary criminals.

bread-ration tickets. But that is obviously ridiculous. Alas, the reality is far more serious, so serious that I am keeping it from everybody, even from my friends, even from my sisters . . . even from myself.

In spite of everything, I had almost believed the various stories; so that my father's phone-call just now, telling me they're in the Cherche-Midi[13] came as a terrible shock. My father[14] had heard it from his friends in the police, who pass on information to him wherever he happens to be hiding. André is apparently there under his *real name*. At six o'clock there was a second phone call from Papa. It seems that when they were arrested they were taken to the Gestapo, in the Rue des Saussaies,[15] and from there, secretly, to the Cherche-Midi. They think André hasn't been questioned yet. And now? What next? Will they interrogate them? Will there be a military tribunal? A trial? What will the sentence be? Were they armed?

Raymonde is so wound up, her eyes are blazing, shining, with dark shadows round them. She has just told me that according to her informant (but is it true?) the twelve who were in the building where my cousin Paule was nearly

13 A French military prison from 1851 until 1947. At 54 Boulevard Raspail, it was evacuated in 1940 and used from 1940–44 by the German Occupation army to house political prisoners.

14 Jules Perquel (1871–1953): Jacqueline's father, a banker and founder of the newspaper *Le Capital*, had been living in hiding in central Paris, with false identity papers.

15 11 Rue des Saussaies was the Gestapo headquarters in the VIIIe arrondissement of Paris.

arrested four days ago, some of them foreigners, Dutchmen,[16] have already been shot. Oh my God! I pray for them. Their task was terrifying: to make contact with German soldiers in order to extract information and persuade them to desert.

André doesn't have a clean shirt. Has he had anything to drink? Or anything to eat? Is he able to get any sleep? Prison nights must be so long and so terrible. Will he be . . . ill-treated?

People talk about the things they do to them, the state they're in when they're taken back to their cells. My body turns to ice when I think about it. I pray for him. But I don't even know if I believe in God. Not every day, alas. And especially not every night. I call out to God, but do I believe in Him? I no longer know who or what to hold on to: what god, what human face, which of the values that used to give meaning to my life. Where can I find strength, hope, a moment of oblivion?

It would seem that nothing remains of our old life, our peaceful life. Over the months and years we have got used to the horrors taking place – people being arrested, whole families disappearing at a stroke – and daily life has become a mixture of squalor and tragedy with the occasional bizarre comic moment; and then there are the vegetables to be prepared (endless green beans for us), in a strange kitchen

16 Members of a Dutch resistance group that operated during the Nazi occupation of the Netherlands. Led by a Dutch Christian, Joop Westerweel, and a Jewish German refugee Joachim Simon, the group was founded in August 1942. From 1943 they worked with the OJC in Paris.

where the cat sleeps in the warmth and I help Suzon sweep and keep an eye on the saucepans because Nana is too busy at the back of her peculiar shop, where the comings and goings are both mysterious and oddly familiar and remind me of where we used to live in the Rue de Seine[17] – lots of young people talking in hushed tones, handsome young men, others less good-looking, and young ladies from the Resistance who rush about, type, deliver letters, and wait in cafés and métro stations for the better-looking boys from the network in a complex mixture of sincerity and chaos, escapism, vanity and courage. Where does the truth lie in all of this? Some display an exaggerated degree of patriotism, others none at all; so many of our fellow countrymen have only ever thought about money, yet brave French men and women are being tortured. In this extraordinary mixture of heroism, indifference and cowardice, in the midst of so much uncertainty, confusion and wretchedness, what is one to believe? Sometimes it's easy: the good, the bad, the guilty, the innocent. At other times it's all a muddle.

So what is it to be truly alive? Is it when all our different selves at last cohere into a whole, so that realism and romanticism together create a kind of fluid harmony between the self and the world, between the self and the unconscious, between the self . . . and God? To be truly alive mean having to make choices.

To be truly alive, is also, quite simply, to love.

17 Rue de Seine was the Amars' home towards the end of the war, where members of André's network would meet.

SAME DAY. MIDNIGHT

The air is heavy tonight and stiflingly close. It must be going to rain. There hasn't been a single clear night all summer, just endless dark clouds blown in by the cold west wind from the Normandy coast.

My darling, where are you? What are you thinking about in your cell, if that is where you are this dark night? Are you asleep? Why am I haunted by ghosts from the past tonight? I can't sleep. I keep thinking about our holidays, so long ago now, your holidays and mine, the two of us together. Do you remember? Lazy days, bittersweet, undeserved, shimmer in my mind, like the wings of a butterfly. My night is scattered with the golden pollen dust of memory, glimmers of light from the past, undimmed, and filled with your presence. I am escaping into the past tonight, with you. Do you remember?

Do you remember Brioni, the small green island in the Adriatic, and the ships lying motionless in the sea, their great sails painted, as they might have been in Ancient Greece, violet or saffron, like Ulysses's ships in Ithaca? And do you remember sailing slowly down the Corinth Canal and the bank covered in asphodels, and Aphrodite's temple at Delphi, with its marble columns looming up in the dawn light, the same tawny colour as the earth you loved so much? And the stones of Mycenae, and the theatre at Epidaurus, hidden in the curve of the wild hillside. The land of Pallas Athena, 'the scarlet shroud wherein the dead gods lie', where so much blood is now being spilt.

Et la Grèce, ma mère, où le miel est si doux
Argos, et Ptéléon, ville des hécatombes,
Et Messa la divine, agréable aux colombes . . .[18]

And do you remember Venice at night, in the moonlight, more beautiful, and more potent than by day, the buildings sculpted by shadows, the columns and scrolls silver, like a dream far stranger than reality? And Venice in the heat of the day, in her carnival finery, glistening and shimmering like the queens of Byzantium, dressed in royal purple, and dripping with jewels and gold? Venice, where, leaving the gondolas to the tourists, the locals dive down narrow alleyways to the noisy sunlit markets and surge onto the *vaporetto*, while we dream quietly by ourselves in the hidden gardens of the palazzos, in the cool, shady courtyard of the Ca' d'Oro which I loved so much, every stone, every step on the staircase, every corbel imbued with the past.

And do you remember our villa in Deauville, which you too came to love, where I spent every summer from my earliest childhood, where I grew up, lived, loved, and where, one glorious summer, as our adult lives were beckoning, we became engaged? And Montigny-sur-Loing, in the very heart of France, and so dear to our own hearts, with its sleepy river running through the green meadows and the lush June creepers, and our little house there – the houses we've lived in! Every day I would wake to the sounds of summer and be

18 'La Nuit de Mai' by Alfred de Musset.

filled with joy hearing you, on the stairs or in the garden, familiar masculine sounds: shifting your dinghy, turning on your torch, jangling your keys, calling, laughing. And the forest. And our friends. Friends who are far away now, or in prison, or dead, and some who are no longer our friends. And fish shimmering in the clear water, and our lost youth. . .

30TH JULY

The news about the war appears to be quite extraordinary and after four years we are daring to believe it. The Germans are in frenzied retreat in Russia. I read in *Le Matin*[19] (what a dreadful paper it is now) that Russian armoured cars are advancing using the same tactics as the Germans did in 1939-40. According to the BBC, having re-taken Vilno and Minsk in the same week, the Russians have crossed the Vistula and are approaching the outskirts of Warsaw. Warsaw again! It was the first city to suffer the misery and destruction that has engulfed Europe, the first to be left in ruins, scene of the first massacre of the war. Now it's facing a bloody liberation.

And now our own cities are being destroyed: Lisieux, Vire, Coutances, Caen, the lovely medieval city that we often used to visit when we were on holiday in Deauville in the old days. In Normandy, Montgomery's armies have not yet taken

19 Founded in 1884, by 1914 *Le Matin* was one of the four biggest daily newspapers in France. Nationalist and anti-Communist in tone, it openly approved of collaborationist policies in 1940, and adopted a pro-Nazi line.

Troarn, nor Saint-André-sur-Orne, where the battle is still raging.

1ST AUGUST

I met Nadine at 6 o'clock this evening at the Café du Critérion. She looked pale and tired. We always meet in one of the cafés around the Gare Saint-Lazare or the Place de l'Opéra so as not to have to walk too far. The métro isn't running at all now. We've been told, for the second time, that the Dutchmen in the building were shot. Apparently they found all kinds of things in their rooms: German uniforms, Gestapo identity papers and guns. According to one of the group, André and César are both either at the Cherche-Midi or at Fresnes;[20] according to him they're not likely to be executed, and will probably get away with being deported. But what does he know? Could it be true? Are the Germans really bothering with enquiries? Proper enquiries? Can we possibly be *hoping* for deportation? But that's how it is. How impossible it is to share fear; it cuts one off from everyone.

Meanwhile, I carry on doing my hair and making up my face. I put on my flowered dress and I do the shopping. I go to the crooked grocer on the corner of the Rue de Moscou: he's young and flirtatious, with an eye for the ladies, definitely

---

20 The second largest prison in France, 10km south of Paris: members of the French Resistance, and British SOE agents, were imprisoned there during the war. Prisoners were held in horrific conditions, more often than not tortured. Many died there.

no sort of hero, and he makes a fortune selling his black market butter and cheese. I watch Nana's tireless activity with admiration, and I go on living. What a betrayal, leading a parallel life while you are locked up, I don't know where or what it's like, or even if . . . How can I bear this sham, how can I carry on talking, how can I carry on living? There's a lot going on at the back of the shop. . . On the whole they take it very seriously, with a few lighter moments of course! Several thousand FFI[21] Northern Zone armbands are hidden here, as well as papers, and files, and several radio transmitters in the cellar.

Nana receives all sorts of visitors in the back of the shop, or on the first floor: her handsome young 'clients', a few old 'aunts', or elderly 'cousins', perfectly respectable old ladies who decipher telegrams and know the codes. There are some young women who do amazing things, like wonderful little Zaki, who has eyes like a cat and is calm and beautiful, a sweet child from the Balkans who appeared out of nowhere and ended up in the Maquis with the Resistance, and now lives at Nana's. And then there are other girls who go around on bicycles, or on one of the few trains still running, or even in Boche lorries, or peasants' hay carts, smiling nicely, carrying innocent-looking cheap suitcases, the contents of which would get them shot on the spot. I may be imagining it, but it seems to me that the prettiest and most elegant of the girls rarely undertake any missions. Of course, in this environment, there

---

21 *Forces Françaises de l'Intérieur* was the formal name used by Général de Gaulle, in the later stages of the war, for French Resistance fighters.

are all sorts. Some people are actually afraid: the poor wretches have to wind each other up before they can do anything; there are a few show-offs, and even some snobs, the type who say things like 'Général de Gaulle and I . . . .' or 'I have a hot line to London' or 'My orders come from the British Army.' There are also any number of modest men and women who work hard and say nothing. In the midst of it all, Nana remains magnificent. She won't tolerate any squabbling, and she'll do anything: she goes round the prisons, she knows the nuns, the nurses, the chaplains; she carries parcels, and delivers messages around the network; she takes on all causes, and does it all for France. She is driven by ambition, pride and a passionate sense of honour, like a *sans-culotte*,[22] or a Chouan[23] of the olden days. She hasn't the slightest interest in money; she's gruff, generous and quick-tempered, dismissing all and sundry with 'If you're not happy, you can just b***** off'. There's no such thing as simple heroism. Of course she loves it really. She loves the action, the danger: it satisfies some deep-rooted need in her, a longing for drama and glory, a certain craving to be part of a wider circle (frustrated until now but for which she is certainly cut out), all mixed with an intense desire to be of service, to sacrifice

22 A largely urban movement of the labouring poor, shopkeepers and artisans who played a central role in the early years of the French Revolution. The name refers to the fact that, unlike the bourgeois revolutionaries who wore fashionable silk knee breeches (*culottes*), the working classes wore *pantalons* (trousers).
23 Members of a mostly peasant, Royalist insurgency movement in Western France 1793–1800.

herself, and a complete indifference to death. There are no chinks in Nana's patriotism, it is total, passionate, innocent, sublime. I am not always fully in tune with it, nor is Suzon. But thank God there are still people like her in France. As long as Nana exists, there must be others like her. Her son is with de Gaulle in Morocco. She hasn't heard from him.

2ND AUGUST

Still not a word. I can't stop thinking about how our men have been sacrificed. So much blood is still being spilt, in prisons, under torture, during hideous German reprisals. It's being spilt in cells and in cellars, and in the countryside, and along the roads of the Ain, the Creuse, the Corrèze, the Dordogne, all over France. This is the blood of our boys, proudly wearing their armbands, their belts hung with grenades and sub-machine guns, smiling and young and full of hope. It's their life-blood. What good will it do for our country? Do the Allies know? Are they grateful? And, in the end, will their blood save the honour of France? This is the blood of our friends, will it *really* bring us all closer to victory? And what if it doesn't? What if we can't be certain? What if it's being spilt for nothing?

Talked about all that over lunch in a bistro on the Rue d'Anjou, where Marie-Rose and MC had taken me. They are wonderful friends to have in these grim times. Marie-Rose is a sceptic. But then you would have to be prepared to bring up your sons to the age of twenty for nothing, to believe in *nothing*, to retain a sense of the absurd, as well as a sense of proportion, in the midst of the present drama; you would

have to hold fast to your intellect, to your talents and your happiness; you would somehow have to keep all this alive for an uncertain future, a distant light at the end of a long tunnel. Would it amount to more than saving your own skin? Is that what being a human being amounts to? That can't be true, however it might appear. It all depends on the particular moment, I think. Sometimes I have faith, at other times not. It goes up and down. There is a time for doubt, for scepticism, when your thoughts are in free play – human consciousness needs that freedom; and then there comes a time when you must make a choice, when you must put away doubt and fight, when, if you are truly human, you know in your heart what is right. In spite of everything, I think I still believe in that.

6TH AUGUST

Tonight on the radio on the 'Le Quart d'heure de l'Europe'[24] at 10.30: 'The Americans have reached the Loire, between Saint-Nazaire and Nantes, they are on the outskirts of Brest; Brittany is cut off. American armoured divisions have taken Laval and Mayenne and are heading towards Paris.' Have I heard right? My heart seems to miss a beat. We all look at each other. There is complete silence in the room.

We've waited for four years to hear those words!

---

24 Possibly the 15-minute programme called 'Les Français parlent aux Français' which was broadcast by the BBC every day from 14th July 1940 to 31st August 1944.

MIDNIGHT

The faces this evening will remain etched on my mind for the rest of my life: of people brought together by the war and by fate, gathered in that little room with its faded yellow wallpaper and an old sideboard full of mismatched china (from Nana's years as a concierge) and all of us, my motley group of companions in misfortune, have clung to the same raft, been tossed by the same storm, and faced the same perils – a random group which will probably be driven apart in time, but at that moment, together, we had our first sight of dry land. . . .

I remember . . . I remember May 1940, June 1940, Paul Reynaud's speech, 'France cannot die', and the communiqué that followed: 'The enemy's advance forces have reached Forges-les-Eaux.' These were the tanks, those famous tanks of the Panzer Divisions, which had to be allowed to pass, alone, in the vanguard, with no supplies, and no infantry, like General Huntziger's *enfants perdus*.[25] Our long journey began at dawn, in the rain, on 11th June.

The last evening for Sylvie and me at Montigny-sur-Loing when the village 'elders' were beating the forest of Fontainebleau with torches and shotguns hunting down

25 Charles Huntziger (1880 –1941) was a French general during WWI and WWII. During the German invasion of France in 1940 he held field command of the 2nd Army; stationed in the Ardennes, his troops failed to hold the line when German tanks attacked unexpectedly near Sedan. The French phrase *enfants perdus* is used for soldiers sent on a particularly dangerous mission.

parachutists: there was old Chauvin, with his amazing moustache, who had fought in 1914–18, and our neighbour Monsieur Martin, who was dying of fright. . . . The sound of women whispering, while the deliriously patriotic Madame Michel repeated over and over again, as she wiped her hands on her apron, 'France has never been beaten.'

Our last night in the small house by the river, saying goodbye to my parents in the garden, as the day dawned on our defeat, both of them so anxious and so sad, my mother in her big shawl with her delicate, pale face, my father suddenly old, consumed with worry. We said goodbye to the roses, to the river bank, and to happiness. And you, André, you were fighting God knows where. And I remember the voice of my friend Raymonde, arriving in the early morning, white as a sheet, and saying, 'They're at Ville d'Avray!' . . . And finally the exodus, the same for everyone, a frenzied departure, a frantic flight, people snatching a wicker chair, a saucepan, even a mattress, something from their past, some fragment of their life, and setting out in the hot, unforgiving sunshine. Raymonde was driving the car; the towns were swarming, the hotels full to overflowing; not a bed or a piece of bread to be had anywhere; just the sound of radios blaring out the dreadful news. The Belgian refugees who had taken Poitiers by storm were not letting it go: there wasn't a room to be had; and still that deep blue sky. And suddenly I remember that strangely calm night, at V—— in the heart of Poitou, with the RPs (old friends of my parents) with whom we had sought refuge. Such a peaceful house, in ancient, serene, unspoiled countryside, with all the scents of summer, of gardens and

fields and houses that have been lived in for generations, that are full of old furniture, slightly musty, but smelling of beeswax and of fruit. To be staying there was as extraordinary as everything else, in a real bedroom, with flowered wallpaper, dusted and polished, unchanging, like the rest of the house, inward-looking, steeped in history, far away from the road, from invasions, from battles. Far removed from strangers. Out of time. More than a house, perhaps, a sanctuary: more than a sanctuary, a goal, giving meaning to life: short and quiet as the night was, how deeply I breathed in its milkiness, basking in the cool light of the distant stars, which shone deep into the soil. French soil.

(Strange how some details rise to the surface, and yet they're all part of the same pool of memories: nostalgia for the past mingles with fear for the future, the anxious forebodings that were so much a part of our wanderings.)

The time at Le Pyla, in the absurdly named Villa Soledad (Villa Solitude), the sweet holiday house where I went to stay with my aunt, who was packing her bags and spending the days dashing from one Mairie to another trying to get to England to join her husband. She left one morning with her children; it felt terribly empty after they'd all gone. The house and the garden seemed suddenly very lonely, in the middle of all the chaos, just myself and my daughter and Marie, and a whimpering, terrified grandmother who didn't understand what was happening. But I stayed there, alternately anxious and resentful, while my daughter, dressed in pink, went to the beach with Marie, who wore white and looked like a smart nanny. And I spent our 'holiday' in the

sun-baked Landes, mulling over the defeat, the extent of the disaster, the lack of news, walking back and forth over the pine needles that carpeted the garden, waiting, hoping, praying, stupidly, for a miracle: some crazy battle on the Loire, such as Charles Martel fought,[26] or for some new Saint Geneviève[27] to rise up on the banks of the Dordogne. And still there was no news of André, at Forbach[28] or on the Somme, or – I knew not where. No news, either, of our friends who had scattered all over the country, or of my parents who were somewhere on the road. . . . I spent some terrible days searching for news in Bordeaux, which was crawling with people. I would go there by car with Raymonde, my mainstay and comfort, almost the only one, apart from Yvonne N, who was living in a hotel nearby. All the government ministries were pouring in, unpacking their files on the pavements; the *préfecture* was besieged: there was panic, mad hysteria, and there was cowardice too. It was an awful time, and shameful. A whole country was foundering there in the streets and hotels, like a latter-day Pompeii, burning under the lava that was Germany, and the full horror of it brought out the worst in people. Some were blatantly indifferent, while

26 Charles Martel (c.688–741) known to all French schoolchildren as the hero whose forces overcame the army of the Umayyad Caliphate at Tours in 732, thereby halting the conquest of Western Europe by the Muslim invaders. Modern historians are divided over the significance of the battle.
27 The patron saint of Paris, she saved the city from the Huns in 451 by persuading the people of Paris not to flee but to remain and pray.
28 Forbach: a key French industrial city close to the German border.

others could not hide their fear, nor some, I am sorry to say, their delight. France had fallen. Why, tonight, am I haunted by those faces from the past, and those long-forgotten voices? Voices like that of the officer in a crowded restaurant furiously demanding chicken cooked with morels, 'it's on the menu, dammit!' and another ordering champagne and raising a toast, 'To the Germans! I respect the Germans. But as for those English pigs. . . .' And Pétain's voice, for the first time, on the wireless, that trembling old man's voice announcing the armistice. And our tears. Already, of course, worrying remarks were being slipped in. And already, even among my acquaintances, people were beginning to show their true colours, to talk differently: it was becoming fashionable to use certain words, while others were quietly forgotten. The 'Huns' became the 'Germans', then the 'enemy', then simply, 'they'. All the time, in the heat of this erupting volcano, one man was toiling away in the shadows; his name was heard more and more frequently, until it was on everybody's lips, 'Laval . . . Laval . . . Laval'[29], spoken with the instinctive, servile respect that people show for someone who has been chosen by Destiny.

I can still hear them, sitting here alone this evening, like a distant diminuendo, all jumbled up, voices from my days in Bordeaux which will die with me. Poor Madame EB (convinced that she, more than anyone, was being hunted because of her husband's newspaper) with her silver fox furs and her

---

29 Pierre Laval was head of the Vichy government from April 1942 to 19th August 1944, and was the main architect of the policy of co-operation with Nazi Germany.

over-made-up mouth and her suitcases: 'I need a car to take me to Spain, immediately. I must get to the border, with all my luggage, by this evening.' The parliamentary deputy who said over and over again, 'Albert Lebrun[30] slunk away like a common servant. Laval had him caught in quarter of an hour. He completely collapsed.' The bizarre, shrill, outburst of a woman, the brilliant wife of a then minister and a close acquaintance, whom I had always considered to be charming, pleasant and liberal, who suddenly, and for no discernible reason, began raving, telling me that there was to be a pogrom the next day. 'Yes. Right here. Get away, now. The French are planning a pogrom here in the streets of Bordeaux!' (I thought her suggestion outrageous and ignored it.) She went around repeating it to anyone who would listen, first of all for the benefit of the old-established Jews (the richest): 'I've got them scared. They're leaving in droves. It's such fun.' And so a great many people were able to escape, in some cases to her great satisfaction.

Nor can I forget the composure of my father, who remained near Poitiers, where he was staying with our friends the RPs. His calm words were relayed to me: 'I'm quite all right, I'm taking things gently – my knee is giving me a spot of bother at the moment.' (So there were some people who didn't spend their days at the *préfecture* in Bordeaux.)

---

30 Albert Lebrun (1887–1963), President of France 1932–1940, was replaced by Pétain as Head of State in 1940; he fled to the Isère, where he was captured in August 1943, briefly imprisoned and subsequently kept under surveillance. In August 1944 he acknowledged the leadership of Général de Gaulle.

Then there was the first time I heard someone refer to Pétain simply as 'le Maréchal', and the first time I heard someone mention 'de Gaulle', a name which was almost unknown at the time but which lit up the horizon like a beacon and, spreading wider and wider, unfurled like a flag. The first time someone talked about 'Gaullists'! That was glorious.

And one day the dry, clipped tone of that monster of an airman (without an aeroplane), faceless as far I was concerned, with his vile talk that I shan't ever forget. He didn't know me, but said, as we sat watching the coming and going in the lobby of the Hôtel de Grande Bretagne, 'If it were up to me, none of those Rothschilds, none of those Jews would get far. I'd confiscate their visas, and their passports and I'd force them to stay exactly where they are. They're the people responsible for the war. Just look at them. I can spot them even from behind.' 'But not from in front!' I snapped. And then out came the usual idiotic platitude: 'Not you of course, I didn't mean you. You're different, you're the wife of a French officer!' Nearby I could see the sad, beautiful face of the Baroness Robert de R, who was leaving, in despair, without her sons, who were lost somewhere at the Front, and I shouted at him, and yes, to my shame, I said all those stupid, humiliating things that I was to repeat over and over again, pathetic proof of national loyalty, a grim and pointless tally of our dead and wounded, laid before judges not worthy of the name. 'You want names of officers' mothers, officers' wives? Lists of dead and wounded? Here, take them! Is that enough? You want more? How many more do you need?'

At last, thanks to the efforts of Yvonne N, one day there was a telephone call telling me that André was safe and well.

I got the news in Bordeaux, where Sylvie and I had ended up in lodgings, at the back of a strange old provincial house. Just to know he was alive, was thinking of us! I was drunk with joy. For a brief moment time stood still.

And then there was the first time I heard English radio, in the Corrèze, in a house belonging to an old peasant woman: she was wearing a straw hat and busying herself with the saucepans on her kitchen range, listening intently – she flicked off the wireless when Vichy radio came back on. (Other remarks come to mind: S my sister-in-law asking, 'Do you know what they did to the Jewish women in Poland?' or Yvonne, in the car, saying, 'Did you know that in Germany all able-bodied Jewish men between the ages of eighteen and fifty-five are being put into camps?')

Vichy! In July 1940 Vichy was swarming with people. I had managed to get there, with my daughter, and I tracked down my father-in-law – the banks had moved there – who was living in a miserable little suburban villa – the Villa Parva; yet even though it was the graveyard of the Republic, the end of the world we had known, Vichy provided a shelter of sorts. A new era was beginning on the back of the tragedy of France: some people were already going under, swept away in the maelstrom of history, while others rushed in, regrouped, and were happy to use the defeat to their own advantage. The defeat of France would be lived out, day after day, night after night, like a love affair.

In the middle of all the confusion, in the narrow summer streets and overcrowded hotels, in parks and at the spa, all those haggard eyes, those faces glowing with acquiescence;

those who could see which way the wind was blowing walked with bent backs and servile smiles; others strutted along full of self-importance, having already obtained positions for themselves.

An acquaintance from the Béarn, TV, swaggered about thoroughly pleased with himself, already well-adapted to the new situation, exclaiming, 'My dear, your husband was an absolute hero. As it happens we were together, in the self-same spot. Pity more of "your" chaps weren't of that calibre.' The 'good mornings' became more reserved, the greetings more tight-lipped, the handshakes less firm. So quickly! And all around the Parc des Sources, on the main square, with its pathetic holiday bunting, a crowd of eager courtiers besieged the Majestic Hotel, where the Old Man slumbered on his throne.

The hollow sound of Vichy, the overcrowded and turbulent home of the National Assembly. Any number of my father's friends were there, men I had met in the past with him, round his dining room table (senators, deputies, journalists). Some showed strength and courage from the beginning. Others, white with fear at first, decided after a few days, when the colour had returned to their cheeks, to move with the times, which is to say they went to see Laval. The overriding fear for many of them was that they might not be needed and would be forgotten. In the middle of all the uncertainty and controlled panic, and the feeling of having been abandoned by the government, at a time when my heart was breaking and my life was in turmoil, at a time when one could be certain of nothing, some friends remained – and I have not forgotten them.

There was Henri Lémery,[31] whose Créole gentleness was such a comfort (in spite of the fact that he was one of the Maréchal's oldest friends, he quickly, and sadly saw the way things were going). And there was always Raymonde's laughter, delightful and so much needed, and G's affectionate teasing: thank God for them. Anatole Monzie's friendship was like a soothing balm; he was a handsome Southerner, with a warm voice and a fine, outstretched hand. I loved his 'Bonjour Jacqueline!', and his gift for life, his way of speaking and his humour. I can picture him now, in Vichy, in the lobby of the Ambassadors, on the shady little terrace, or at home in Paris, sitting in his study or in his little courtyard; I can see his tall, aristocratic profile, his walking sticks propped beside him, his velvet jacket, his beret perched unsteadily on his oddly bumpy head; behind his glasses, his eyes were unforgettable, full of life and curiosity; above all, I remember his radiant charm. Yet, in spite of my Gascon friend's great intelligence – a little lacking perhaps in intuition and common sense – his star was waning.

'Will my friends protect me from my ancestors?' was the question I often asked myself.

I remember, too, the furious torrents of invective let loose by Caillaux,[32] the elderly President of the Council (his anger,

---

31 Henry Lémery (1874–1972): born in Saint-Pierre, he was the first native of Martinique to hold political office in France, serving under Clémenceau between 1917 and 1920. Briefly Minister for the Colonies under Pierre Laval, he quickly distanced himself from him, while remaining close to Pétain.

32 Joseph-Marie-Auguste Caillaux (1863–1944) was prime minister of France from 1911–1912.

as is often the case with very old men, would turn out to be short-lived), with the toughness that had been a feature of his indomitable youth. 'If we break from England, we will have to live with the disgrace for 150 years!' he piped in his falsetto voice, puffing out his elegant little chest, like a man who was used to a fight. . .

So much talk, snatches of conversation, words surfacing from nowhere . . . my head is full of them tonight. I remember a buzz of voices from the past, at the Cintra, the chic outdoors bar where the Vichy crowd used to meet in 1940, or in the park, in the sunshine of that remarkable, yet cruel summer, the summer of our defeat – or on the banks of the Allier, at dusk, under a halo of rosy light, when the green grass was streaked with gold by the late-setting sun: such a beautiful summer, unforgettable and doomed.

Alibert's[33] words as reported to us: 'I am drawing up some detailed laws for *them*.' And, worst of all, what M said, so casually, on a sunny afternoon at the swimming pool, a grim remark which cut like a dagger in my heart: 'I am reliably informed that everything is ready to invade England. Hitler is only waiting for his meteorologists to confirm that the weather is set fair for three days.' I looked at the cloudless sky. Set fair for three days.

---

33 Raphael Alibert (1887–1963) Minister of Justice, in July 1940 he instituted a review of naturalisations since 1927, as a result of which 15,000 'French' men and women had their citizenship revoked. He published the first *Statut des Juifs* in October 1940, excluding Jews from a number of Civil Service posts.

Why this rush of memories tonight, when the first major victory, and the closest, has been announced – the Allies advancing on Paris? Why this sudden flood? These ghosts from the past have risen up, randomly, have appeared unsummoned, and they will disappear again, into oblivion, and will remain there.

Why tonight, of all nights, when for the first time we have reason to hope, why remember it all now? All that we have lived through, day after day, hour after hour, the tragedy of it all, the tragedy of the Jews, our tragedy, my tragedy.

Despite ourselves, being Jewish has become even more of an obsession than being French, an obsession which, like a hidden wound, has worked its way slowly and insidiously under our skin and right into our souls. Little by little it has made us into 'foreigners' in our own country, French but 'different', stealthy, excessively humble or over-assertive, constantly on edge. It has turned us into outsiders, always on the move, jobless, linked together by unspoken ties of complicity and fear.

At first life in the Unoccupied Zone seemed to carry on as normal. We pretended to be like everyone else, yet every day the propaganda continued, from the Paris newspapers, German radio, even Vichy radio, which swiftly fell into line; all those names that I would rather forget, voices that I never want to hear again; we were insulted and spat on; we had filth thrown at us, onto our elegant pre-war bourgeois clothes, thrown at veterans of the First World War, at our fathers, with their medals and their blue army tunics. Pitiful accoutrements, pathetic, silent pleas.

And then that strange, divided life, almost entirely idle. And also, at the beginning, our incomprehension and our

refusal to 'understand', together with the shameful reactions of so many of us. I can still hear the distinguished voice of Monsieur S, an industrialist from eastern France, in the garden of the hotel in Vichy, expressing his astonishment at the first *Statut des Juifs*. 'It's quite absurd. These measures can't be intended for the French, for French Jews! For foreign Jews perhaps, but not French Jews! It's inconceivable! This is robbery.' Poor Monsieur S. It was much worse than that. They took everything we owned, they took away our jobs, and worst of all they took away our citizenship, our deeply valued position in society achieved with such difficulty over the past three-quarters of a century. And then, bending to German pressure, they took our freedom, and, finally, they took our lives.

The shock of the first arrests in Paris in '41 shattered the illusory peace of that fine summer: they arrested Pierre Masse – I can see him now, with his calm face, looking like a blond Confucius, full of wisdom, so perceptive, so French – and Jean-Jacques Bernard, and other well-known figures. My cousin A should have been in the same round-up but miraculously managed to escape, slipping out of his building in an act of amazing audacity while five Gestapo henchmen were already in his flat dividing up his belongings. My brother-in-law was arrested, interned in Dijon, Beaune-la-Rolande, Pithiviers, and then Drancy.[34] Drancy, that terrible name that haunts our lives. We would get news of the arrests by telephone. 'Cécile

34 Situated in the North-Eastern suburbs of Paris, Drancy was a detention centre for Jews awaiting deportation to the extermination camps. Between 1942 and 1944, 67,400 French, Polish and German Jews, including 6000 children, were deported from Drancy.

and her son are ill. They're in the same "clinic" as Paul.' And then there were the massive deportations: 'they need a thousand', 'they need fifteen hundred'. And the round-ups, more and more round-ups: round-ups in the XIe arrondissement, the round-up of foreign mothers and children, taken kicking and screaming, or throwing themselves out of windows. They were dragged to the Vél d'Hiv,[35] where what took place was more appalling than anything anyone had ever witnessed. It was 16th July 1942. The city was reduced to silence, struck dumb with the horror of it. Even the 'collaborators' were shocked to the core.

And little by little we became 'separate', cut off from all civic life, and slowly the suffering grew worse . . . We were turned into Jews, gradually, from outside, we who had forgotten our Jewishness. They struck at the heart of our prosperous, middle-class identity, in which we had felt so secure after the Dreyfus affair.[36] We had grown deaf to the outside world,

35 The Vélodrome d'Hiver was an indoor cycling track close to the Eiffel Tower. Following a round-up carried out for the Germans by the French Milice on 16th and 17th July 1942, 13,000 Jews were taken there: 5,500 were women, over 4,000 children. Having been held for five days in appalling conditions, the prisoners were taken to internment camps at Drancy, Beaune la Rolande and Pithiviers.

36 Alfred Dreyfus (1859–1935), a Jewish army captain, was convicted in 1894 of treason for allegedly selling military secrets to the Germans, on the basis of a document later found to have been forged. The case attracted widespread public attention, splitting France into Dreyfusards, who sought his exoneration, and anti-Dreyfusards, for whom Dreyfus symbolised the disloyalty of French Jews. The split, which set left against right, produced a lasting impact on the nation. He was pardoned in 1899 and finally exonerated in 1906.

at ease in the country we thought of as ours, living in our comfortable houses, sitting in our directors' chairs, in our banks and shops, on company boards. And then something mysterious, atavistic, rose up from deep in our souls, as if such misery was something which we had always been used to. Normal life had come to an end, and wandering and flight became our daily bread. We were transformed into outlaws, pariahs, beggars, desperate for a shred of security, for a share in our native country.

And yet life goes on of course, and we carried on living. Nothing is constant, not even misery. We were forever packing up, leaving, taking train after train after train, moving on for reasons that were not always clear, sometimes just to alleviate the tedium of waiting, to break the monotony, or simply to prove that we still could move around, in the ever tightening net of the Unoccupied Zone, which was shrinking by the day. We went to Marseille, to Nice, to Grenoble, to Toulouse, to Aix-les-Bains, even to Paris, poor, fretful travellers, vulnerable passengers on a dangerous, possibly deadly journey. We appeared calm and relaxed, like everyone else, when we reached a demarcation line, at Moulins, or elsewhere, or at stations packed with Germans or French Milice,[37] hung with huge signs reading 'No Jews Allowed'. We carried on smiling, clutching our pathetic forged papers in our pockets, papers which would

37 A paramilitary force created in January 1943 by the Vichy regime with German aid, to fight against the Resistance. Made up of native Frenchmen, their local knowledge made them more of a threat than the Germans to the *résistants*. The Milice were also used to round up Jews and *résistants* for deportation.

not have withstood close inspection, looking straight ahead, while our hands trembled and our hearts pounded.

And so, one day, I arrived back in Paris. It was as if I had found my soul again, my very being. Paris was empty, huge, silent; there was no traffic, apart from 'their' fast cars. But I was back in Paris, where I had walked so often in my dreams, and where I had to stop myself from kissing the cobblestones and the squares and the grey stones of the buildings. I was able to see my parents again: for some thirty years they had lived in the same place, and now they had been forced to go into hiding. My father was being hidden by his old cook in a tiny flat in Montmartre, in a narrow little street where everyone referred to him as 'the gentleman'. He would step out with his stick in the morning, somewhat disguised (or so he believed), wearing a cap and not so many medals. He saw almost no one from his old life, apart from two or three friends and my mother, who was worn out by the endless coming and going on the métro but still elegant and beautiful and still, by some miracle, living in her own apartment, protected by her Italian nationality.[38] The Gestapo had called on her five or six times: with their revolvers at the ready, their feet on the furniture and their cigars stuck in their mouths, they had hurled insults at her, demanding to see my father, while she held her ground, weeping with heroic artlesssness. 'He's gone. He's left me. He's run off. I'm all alone.'

---

38 JM-A's mother (1886–1972) was Hélène (Ellen) Allatini. Her family had lived in Salonika but had Italian citizenship and was originally from Livorno and Florence.

Meanwhile, my parents contrived as far as possible to live a normal life and to adapt to the new circumstances. They were creatures of habit, almost military in their routine, and their days continued to follow the same pattern: a trip to the shops, a siesta, an occasional outing to the cinema. That had always been their way and they made few concessions to the outside world or to events, apart from one thing: their whole life now centred on the daily English radio broadcast. Meanwhile everything around them was changing. My brother-in-law had been arrested, my cousins in the Unoccupied Zone were scattered, our friends had left or, worse, had already been arrested and deported; and when my older sister, who had raced over to meet me the day I arrived, suddenly raised her arm to pick up the phone, I noticed a strange patch of embroidery stitched onto her dark blouse, which didn't go at all with her outfit. Horrified, I realised it was the barbaric yellow star: it was the first time I had seen one. And in a silent, empty and disdainful Paris, there was no dust, but nor was there any bread, or potatoes, or meat; and the queues in front of the shops began stretching out at dawn; after the terrible cold of the previous winter I watched the glorious rebirth of spring in all its beauty. As for 'them', 'they' were everywhere, in the streets, in the métro, in cafés and in theatres, wearing their field-grey uniform, or the officer's black greatcoat, powerful and alone, always alone, while all around them the hungry crowd swirled, mutely hostile. The elegance of some Parisian women was almost provocative; walking, cycling or travelling on the métro wearing fashionably wide hats with veils and platform shoes and bright

lipstick, deliberately nonchalant as they stared coldly ahead. These women perfectly embodied the unbending soul of Paris, which had never been more beautiful, the silent stiffening at the heart of the city – give or take a few rare moments of excess at Maxim's or the Racing Club or the Opéra. They symbolised the deep underlying layers of Parisian hostility, the unforgettable defiance of Paris under the Occupation.

And then I returned to my increasingly dangerous life in the Unoccupied Zone. I started moving around again, travelling all over the Midi and then the Savoie, where I came across the first young men to be conscripted for the STO.[39] Waiters, shop assistants, hoteliers' sons joined the Maquis, forming the first kernels of the Resistance. They were leaving home for a life of constant fear.

Like so many others, I liked my safe havens and felt curiously at home in some of them; also I learnt to appreciate the beauty of France more than I ever had in peacetime. There were times when I was drunk with the sheer pleasure of still being alive. I loved Marseille: I loved our hideous little flat over the chocolate shop on the Avenue du Prado, I loved the market and the shops, the lilting voices in the echoing air, the southern humour, the noise, the light, the pale glow at dusk over the Old Port. I loved the distant blues and greens

39 *Service du Travail Obligatoire*, the Compulsory Labour Scheme introduced in February 1943 initially required all men aged 20–22 to be deported to work in Germany. This would later be expanded to include men from 16 to 45. Some avoided it by enlisting in the Milice, others by joining the Maquis, the rural guerilla group of the Resistance.

of the Savoie, so deeply imbued with romanticism, the time-less beauty of the shores of the Lac du Bourget on a clear morning, the neat lines of the plane trees stripped of leaves by the autumn winds. I loved the dryness of Provence, the little village in the Vaucluse where, from time to time, we visited our friends Lise and André (like us, under threat) and sat under the big fig tree in their courtyard; I loved the deep September skies.

Yes, we lived with rare intensity, because life was short, although at other times it was as if we had all the time in the world to breathe the clear air – free and pure and safe, like a gift from God and, worn out by our precarious existence, we lay and gazed up at the sky and let the sun soak into our aching bodies.

Yet we couldn't avoid hearing what some of the 'others' were saying, dreadful, idle remarks, dropped from the mouths of our enemies, a mixture of hypocrisy and triumphalism. We came across them everywhere, at the chemist's, at the baker's, all over the place. 'You see! Those Gaullists have taken a beating in Syria. He's had it now!' . . . 'Your little English friends in Libya, what a disaster! The b****ds have had it!' But we never gave up hope. Every hour, every minute, in the bleakest of times, we hoped against hope. In Aix, still beau-tiful during the long stifling summer of 1941 when all was lost, and through the endless winter of 1941–42, and into the next summer when the Germans were victorious in Africa and in Russia, and even when they invaded the Caucasus and seemed about to take Stalingrad, we went on hoping. Bit by bit we got the news from the BBC: it was our late-night aperitif, the cup

of life that sustained our hope, and we drank it down to the last drop.

Of course we were careless and foolish. We went on seeing our friends, we ate, we dined with them in the countryside, beside the lake and by the sea. Even in Paris. We frightened, and irritated, our protectors with our carelessness; we were in hiding, but that didn't stop us going out. We played bridge, we played with our lives, we lived foolishly, because we had to live, and we even loved . . . But we are always on our guard.

The nights, my nights and those of every single Jew, and our children's nights, are times of fear and weeping. Can this go on forever? Will we ever sleep again in this world?

Dearest, darling A, do you remember our wartime nights, those nights of the Occupation? Do you remember the night in Marseille when 'they' arrived, a whole division marching past in the darkness beneath our windows; how we clung together for safety, listening to the never-ending sound of their boots echoing on the cobbles of the Avenue du Prado, in the rain, heavy army boots, followed by softer, more perfidious boots on the feet of the Gestapo. And do you remember that night in Aix-les-Bains, in that gloomy Villa Moana, on the Avenue du Lac, last summer, not long after the green Gestapo car had driven round and round, up and down the steep streets? Do you remember the sound of the leaves rustling in the garden in the cool early autumn wind, and then, suddenly, in the middle of the night, the ring at the door shattering the silence, and me telling you to escape through the back garden, that at one o'clock in the morning it had to be 'them'? But you went

to the door, you opened it, you opened the door . . . and there was nobody there! It was *nothing*. And dawn at Villa Moana, until 7 or 8 o'clock, deadly hours, until the sun was fully up and spreading its warm glow over the beauty of the Savoie, and over that peaceful garden: do you remember how nothing could assuage that early morning fear, which dissipated quite suddenly, and quite irrationally at around 9 o'clock, as if 'they' never arrived in daylight, as if 'they' never came at lunchtime.

Tonight, too, I am haunted, by the hell of the endless arrests. All around us people were being arrested. First to go was S,[40] my sister-in-law, then your parents and your younger brother.[41] Now you. You are all with me this evening, the absent faces; I can just make you out, all of you, lit up for a moment, then dark, one after another looming palely out of the shadows, into the dying light of my guttering candle. I can see your father's face in the restaurant in Aix, the one on the little Place des Thermes, when we told him that poor S, my sister-in-law, the young mother with two small children, had been taken away by the Italian police. I still see it, that cruel scorching July afternoon, at the Kommandantur in Grenoble, when we tried one last appeal to the authorities to have S released, in that stifling office, where we were questioned by that odious young OVRA[42] (doing a perfect imitation of a Gestapo brute). Your father was normally so calm and so

---

40 Suzie Amar, married to Emmanuel Amar, was born Suzanne Reinach. She was Dreyfus's great-niece.
41 Emmanuel Amar was Andre's brother.
42 *Oeuvre de vigilance et de répression l'antifascisme.*

self-controlled, always courteous and kind, but I remember his face when he thought they were also arresting your younger brother, who was outside in the street waiting for news of his wife: the collapse of such a strong man was devastating, the sudden weakness, his face becoming, unbelievably, in an instant, that of an old man, crumpled, haggard, ashen, overcome by the thought that they might be taking Emmanuel too. His son. And the last time we saw your father before he was arrested, do you remember, when he was already in hiding in the Haute Savoie with your mother and grandmother, but in a poorly chosen spot, with a ludicrously badly-forged identity card and far too much luggage? He had come on his own to dine with us in Aix that evening in October, looking so tired, and so sad, lost in his own thoughts, but his face lit up suddenly when he saw that we had brought our little Sylvio with us. Remember how he smiled, how his voice came to life when he talked to the child, his urgent but somehow pathetic insistence when he said, 'You will come up and see us soon, won't you? We're dreadfully lonely. Mother would be so happy too. When will you come? This week? And will you bring the little one?'

And when we were properly in hiding with our dear friends René A and his wife, in the Savoie, and we heard that on 10th October the Gestapo, fifteen of them, from Grenoble, had gone to the village and arrested your parents: your poor mother who was still ill, so thin and unsteady on her feet in her smart shoes and shivering like an exotic bird, and your eighty-year-old grandmother, barely able to stand on her swollen arthritic legs, in her fine starched organdy blouse, her

white hair beautifully done, and your father extraordinarily calm now that all was lost; the three of them were forced to stand against the wall for hours with all the other Jews in the hotel. We heard how 'they' shouted, and with what pleasure 'they' ransacked the luggage. All the prisoners were taken to Fort Montluc[43] near Lyon. I can still hear the stupid, curt voice of the woman in charge of the Red Cross in Lyon, an elderly spinster, one of Pétain's old maids, a typically frosty automaton of an official, whose answer to my desperately anxious questions was, 'of course they'll receive their parcels, why wouldn't they? Naturally they'll have everything they need. They'll be treated *just like all the others.*' What others, Mademoiselle? Are you blind? Are you deaf? Exactly what others like them have been arrested? An elderly man, an invalid and a very old woman, arrested and treated like criminals, dragged from their home? How many others have you seen treated like that, without even the pretence of a reason? For nothing at all? But we kept quiet, we didn't say any of that to the robots from the Légion or the Milice. What others? Apart from the Jews, what others have travelled that dreadful road of terror, leaving behind them nothing but silence, and our futile rage, our seared hearts? Fort Montluc, Drancy, Auschwitz . . . Who else has struggled along that path?

They were deported on 23rd November. We were in hiding, you and I, in Raymonde's flat, and that night, every time

43 Built as a military prison in 1921, Fort Montluc was used by the Gestapo as a prison, interrogation centre and an internment camp. Over 15,000 people were imprisoned there, of whom 900 were executed, and the remainder transferred to concentration camps.

we heard the whistle of a passing train, we thought they must be in it.

Poor S, where is she now? Alone in her prison in Turin? Where is that beautiful profile, and that wonderful auburn hair which, in summer, she used to wash in the garden in Aix, hair the colour of autumn, shot through with sunlight, magnetic and almost too heavy for her face? Where is she, so full of courage, with her slightly languid voice, and her sudden flashes of joy, her fragile happiness when she was playing with her children? Where are you, Emmanuel, her young husband, and almost a brother to me, arrested in a round-up, for real this time, at the Gare de Perrache in Lyon, at the end of January, and deported via Drancy, humiliated, and mortified to have been taken unarmed. I peer in vain into the shadows for his face, slightly oriental, not unlike that of a young prophet; I look for the warm light of the dark eyes I loved, for the almost tangible vibrancy of his presence; I long to see that tall figure, a prince with his head in the clouds, and once more to enjoy his sparkling, sometimes melancholy humour; I try to picture the drab anorak he was wearing the last time I saw him. But I can see only with my mind's eye, my inner eye. I am blind. And deaf. And finally you, the last to go, and the dearest of all, whose absence is far and away the hardest to bear, where are you tonight? I keep trying to remember your voice, the way you talk, so fast, and your wonderful laugh, but I can't hear them any more. In the dark, I try to visualise the shape of your forehead, your lips, your skin, to smell your hair again . . . I keep trying to capture all these things, your gentle teasing, the feel of your hands, most

of all your warmth, your broad chest and your strong shoulders, your heart beating next to mine, but it's all slipping away. Come back, I beg you. Darling, darling A, try to stay alive.

What have they done to you? Can you hear me? You used to say, 'We won't all be there for the Liberation. Some will be missing.' You're *all* missing.

Have you heard what they're saying this evening? It's what you having been hoping for, for the last four years. 'The Americans sweeping towards Paris.' Is dawn breaking at last?

My God, will it ever be daylight?

7TH AUGUST

Full of hope this morning, a crazy day, bright and warm. The little Place de Clichy, which is so ordinary – and yet so typically Parisian – looks charming, with its spindly trees and its colourful little cafés, despite the presence of large German lorries, camouflaged with yellowing leaves. There are any number of moving gardens in Paris nowadays! Orange awnings and bare-legged girls in floral dresses, everything is glowing, looking somehow Spanish under this new light. It won't be long now.

Everyone is jumpy, people are talking, bicycles are rushing by at top speed, and there's not a policeman in sight. This morning I went into a café to use the telephone and caught snatches of conversation, 'They've nearly reached Le Mans', 'The Germans are retreating South from Caen', 'They announced last night, at 12.30, that Château-Gontier had been taken.' People in the street seem to be waking up at last

from a long sleep, from a series of nightmares, emerging from the shadows of a night that's lasted for four years.

My sister came back out of breath from an errand this afternoon, saying, 'They're at Nogent-Le-Rotrou! I heard it from the Germans' laundress.' Nana returned from one of her numerous 'trysts' saying, 'They've reached Chartres.'

At 7 o'clock someone comes to collect me to go and have dinner in the Rue Saint-Lazare. A glorious sunset lights up the city above the hideous station, and all of a sudden even that seems beautiful. I am dining with Nadine, Félix and my cousin Paule. We have some wine. There is definitely something in the air. The name 'Chartres' spreads like wildfire from table to table, and Dreux and even Vernon. Some German officers at a nearby table are imperturbable, staring into space, eating and drinking in silence. I should imagine this is the last French wine they'll be drinking.

8TH AUGUST

I went to the Tuileries Gardens with my little girl this afternoon. She seems much older than nine. I am worried about her long silences and by the way she glances up at me sometimes, when she thinks I won't notice, trying to understand what's happening. But she doesn't try for long, and soon goes back to the game in which we pretend that we have had 'news' from the Maquis about her *papa*. Then in an instant she becomes her bright, cheerful, trusting self again. The inconstancy of children is truly admirable. Off goes my little Sylvio, with her white hair-ribbon, running about and playing like a

normal child with two little girls of the same age and a little boy, a refugee from Lisieux, who walked from there to Paris. He too has forgotten. They are all running round the big pond, pretending to sail their boats on the water and throwing imaginary balls in the air, playing like children do all over the world, in parks and squares, as if there were no wars or ruins, as if their fathers were still there and would be back for supper, as if death did not exist.

And there we are, Mme L and me, in this beautiful weather, the sun casting a golden glow on the hedges and the lawns which I had never seen at this time of year, until now, until this high-summer, when, after four years, the Germans are finally starting to leave, and I am waiting to hear if my husband is still alive.

We drink some dreadful pink saccharine-sweetened cordials at the kiosk in the Tuileries, in a scene reminiscent of the travelling pastry-seller who gave cornets to all the little girls at Jean-Jacques Rousseau's request. Then we both went and sat on a bench, so that we could watch the children from a distance. Mme L's husband is a prisoner of war, and she has had no news of him since the Battle of Normandy began. He has never seen his youngest daughter. The children are shouting in the distance, in the white dust and the azure haze, running about under the thick canopy of trees, and for a long time, exchanging barely a word, we watch as the pale afternoon light fades. In the sky the swallows are circling, high above, then swirling down to the tops of the trees, as they do in towns everywhere. But this is a scene from *my* city, from Paris, an image of France, both subtle and secret. Surely in the

darkness of your prison, my darling, wherever you are, wherever your dear heart is beating, surely you can see around you the faces of some of those you have loved, perhaps some faces from your life in Paris, shadowy but comforting? France is a tapestry of stones and leaves; trees frame her face like thick locks of hair; prayer inhabits her cathedrals; faith and doubt lie together deep in her soil; she has known defeats and victories, bloodshed and freedom, been at the crossroads of so many ideas, so many battles; her houses and roads and woods all are rooted in history.

Does Mme L's face, her profile, her blue eyes, her calm manner, her strong, practical, hands, do these belong in our country more than my anxious pallor and my taut nerves? Perhaps, but I deserve my place too: I have looked for deeper and more distant echoes, which she has not needed to hear; I have given my spirit, and my faith, and your self-sacrifice, André; like her, I have endured the fate of France, but all along I have borne within me the weight of another, more ancient destiny.

And I look at the woman sitting next to me, who is both like me and not like me: she is attached to this country by roots stretching back into the past and away into the future and, beside her, I feel unsteady and impermanent, a recent arrival from a distant century, with another, hidden face which is also mine, but comes from 'another place', I don't know where, from nowhere; and, in spite of myself, I am also the sister of all these children of Israel whom I don't know, strangers, foreigners, the hunted and the lost, my companions in sorrow, pursued and battered, like me, by the Fate that we share, by the God we have ignored.

And yet, in the midst of the turmoil that is shaking Europe, in a park in Paris, this evening, like so many other evenings, like thousands of other women desperate for news, Mme L and I wait . . . and we wait.

Our hearts are impenetrable; it is increasingly difficult to summon up the whole of a beloved face, one only ever finds fragments of a person and tries to piece them together like bits of a jigsaw, a look, a laugh, a bronzed neck in an open-collared shirt, a holiday pullover, a gesture, the warmth of their skin.

9TH AUGUST

Around the Place de la Concorde, the Rue Boissy d'Anglas,[44] the Hôtel de Crillon[45] and all the other German centres of operation the air is filled with scraps of charred paper falling on our faces, on our hair, on our arms. They've been burning their records, all day long and throughout the night, frantically getting ready to leave.

Everyone now claims to have spotted an Englishman, 'his' Englishman – he had an English accent and blue eyes – who'd been hidden by the concierge, or the grocer, or the neighbour.
. . .

44 11 Rue Boissy d'Anglas served as a German military tribunal during the Occupation.
45 Situated at the end of the Champs Elysées, overlooking the Place de la Concorde, the Hôtel de Crillon was used by the German High Command as their headquarters during the Occupation.

10TH AUGUST

André is at Fresnes. It's definite. He's alive and well. Thank God! Alive and well. I keep repeating the words to myself. They are going round and round in my head. They have lit a thousand lights. He's alive and well. There are no more beautiful words in the world. He's thinking, moving around in his narrow cell, he is suffering; he is thinking, perhaps about me, perhaps about our child, about what's happening. Waiting, hoping, lurching from hope to despair, his mind will be buzzing with worries, from tiny details to profound anxiety, all the absurd chaos and inner turmoil to which all humans are subject. It's absolutely definite. César managed to get word to Nadine, via the mother of a fellow-prisoner, that he's not far away and that they're all well. They never were in the Cherche-Midi.

It's very hard to get a parcel to Fresnes, but Nana has promised to do the impossible, with the help of the chaplain, I think, or one of the nuns, or one or other of her 'old aunts' or 'cousins'. But there is a dark side to everything: I'm afraid now that they will still have time to deport them.

But for the first time, in the dark forest in which I find myself, the forest where Dante wandered, 'midway on life's journey', there is, once more, a glimmer of hope; a flame is burning in my poor heart and I shan't let it die.

12TH AUGUST

My anguish has returned. Nothing helps anguish like this, I feel so alone. Absolutely nothing. The joy of knowing that André is

alive is wrecked a hundred times a day by an endless host of fears, fears that I can barely put into words, even to myself, but which gnaw at me like an octopus with a thousand heads devouring me. We have heard that our men are being interrogated, like murderers, at Gestapo headquarters in the Rue des Saussaies. What questions do they ask? *What* goes on in that place?

My God, at moments I am so afraid, so dreadfully afraid, that I immediately have to suppress the fear, deep inside me, and then I talk, and I do my hair, I put on my lipstick and I go out and meet people, and laugh – for no reason, just to keep on living. Apparently C,[46] a member of the group, an extraordinary character, brave (recklessly so in my opinion) and very high up in the MLN,[47] is no longer with them at Fresnes. What have they done with him? Have they executed him? Apparently the Gestapo thought at first that our men belonged to the group who assassinated Philippe Henriot![48]

Are they at least eating? Are they getting enough of that filthy prison gruel? And enough bread, that black bread?

46 Maurice Cachoud 1916–44, who died after being tortured for two days by the Gestapo at the rue de la Pompe. He told them nothing.
47 MLN: *Mouvement de la Libération*, established at the beginning of 1944 by Philippe Viannay and Claude Boudet, combining the *Mouvements Unis de la Résistance*, of the Southern Occupation Zone, with a number of Resistance movements based in Northern France.
48 A right-wing, Catholic journalist, politician and broadcaster, Henriot (1889–1944) was appointed Secretary of State for Information in 1943. His broadcasts on Radio Vichy earned him the nickname 'the French Goebbels'. He was assassinated in June 1944 by members of the Maquis; the Milice retaliated by assassinating Georges Mandel, an outspoken opponent of collaboration.

What are they doing to them? My God, my God, help him, help me!

No, nothing helps in the dark hours, when one prays out of despair, out of horror, out of emptiness.

Are we worthy of a God we have forgotten, are we worthy even of prayer? Alas, I don't know how to pray: all I am capable of is pleading, screaming, rebelling, railing against God for what He has allowed to happen: so many innocent people have suffered, so much innocent blood has been spilt. I am so unsure of my faith, it is so weak. Even in the darkest hours of the night, when I examine the depths of my soul, I can find none of the mystical fervour of my youth, nor even any belief in country, or in the ideals for which our young men have been fighting, things like justice, the protection of the innocent. I feel that any faith I ever had is dead. And yet at moments it seems to return, only to vanish, and then, when the pain becomes too much, I call out once more, I beg for it to fill this desert, to provide some comfort in this horrible emptiness, but more often than not I don't even understand it any more.

Right now nothing helps, not art, or memories, not beauty, or thinking about the suffering of others, not the hell of Phèdre, nor the blinding of Oedipus, not friends, not anybody. I am torn apart, alone, looking death in the face. Is there nothing for me now but emptiness? And the fear of emptiness?

My heart is weak, my eyes are blind. And yet, somewhere deep inside me, there is still a pale glimmer of hope.

13TH AUGUST

They are saying on the BBC: 'The battle for Paris has reached the outskirts of Chartres.' Wonderful words, the best, the sweetest we could hear. But they don't mean the same for everyone: in August '44 the word 'Liberation' doesn't have the same meaning for everyone, any more than 'Freedom', or 'Hope'. They don't have the same weight, or the same shape; they don't cast the same light. Even place names sound different. Familiar names strike a different chord in every heart: Chartres, Châteaudun, Étampes, Paris.

For the young men in the Resistance groups, in the heart of the Maquis, for the night-train saboteurs, whose faces appeared on 'Wanted' posters stuck up by the Huns on the walls of the métro, the pathetic faces of these 'foreigners' or 'wops', people who had lost everything, who had suffered so much and risked so much, for those who hurled bombs at factories, at military convoys, at V2 runways, for all the night fighters, the fighting men of the secret war, who were captured and now lie in the depths of German prisons, interrogated, tortured (alas, one cannot avoid the word) and who await each dawn behind prison walls, thick walls that no cries can pierce, walls that hide the flow of blood, for all of them, for us, these words, whatever they may be, are war cries, they promise victory. These words mean hope. They mean life.

14TH AUGUST

The heat is heavy, dense, suffocating. Now we often hear gunfire to the west. Where *is* Leclerc's division, where are the Americans? People have seen them at Versailles, at Rueil, at Saint Cloud! But people are seeing all sorts of things in these troubled days. A kind of oppressive silence weighs on the city; the cafés are crowded, but people hardly talk. Parisians are waiting. The women are wearing their light summer dresses, with fashionably full skirts (and fashion still matters), and their hair is loose. Many of the women are beautiful, yet if you look closely you can see their features are drawn, their eyes are feverish and their faces are hollow with nervous exhaustion. The daily struggle to buy food, getting about by bicycle or lorry, work, children, the fight to look after their family, have all left their mark: beneath the make-up lie deep, cruel lines of physical tiredness. Cyclists are racing down the streets, heading who knows where; there's no traffic control. For several days now there hasn't been a policeman to be seen; there is no métro; everyone is getting about on foot; the streets are thick with people; the huge crowds are silent, tense. It is a closed city, cut off, inwardly seething. Will it be freed? Will there be a siege of Paris? Only the birds singing in the trees break the great silence; children play in the squares, and old men doze on benches, oblivious to the madness of the world.

15TH AUGUST

Sylvio's birthday. She is ten today. What a lot she has had to bear in her ten years. How much longer must she bear it? How soon will she forget? Will she ever really forget? Even so we have invited one of her friends to tea, the only one still in Paris, in this heat, and when it's so dangerous. We had the tea party at Maman's: she's still 'in hiding' at her friend's flat in the Rue de Berne. (Not that she's that well hidden – everyone knows she's there, despite her best efforts. The hairdresser in the Rue de Rome recognised her, I think, remembering having done her hair in the past in Deauville. Maman denied it fiercely, but of course it's true. The clandestine life doesn't come naturally to my parents.)

It was a small and sad tea party, so different from parties before the war when my poor little kitten was tiny, the wonderful tea parties at her grandparents' large seaside villa at the height of summer, rather formal, a little tedious, with the whole family, the immaculately turned-out child, and her little friends, smart nannies, and all the beautiful presents laid out on a big table. Those birthday teas seem like a fairy tale from another era. Those days are long past. What has happened to them?

Her friend arrived by bicycle with her mother, who had a headscarf wound around her hair and was heavily made-up and extremely nervous. 'There's bound to be a communist putsch. It's a disaster.' Another friend who was there told us that she was very worried about her husband, who has had to cycle to the tiny village of which he is mayor – a case of *noblesse*

oblige or better late than never (one can vary the proverb). He is, incidentally, a very nice young man.

'Just think, the poor thing had to cycle all the way. I haven't heard a word from him. And it's quite close to the front line. By the way,' she adds, lowering her voice, 'any news of André?' We are whispering . . . The children are playing in an unfamiliar sitting room, small and draped with dust-sheets. I notice Sylvie stiffening slightly as she tries to hear what we are saying, glancing furtively across for a moment, looking both serious and suspicious, before turning back to her friend rather condescendingly, all the while continuing to play at schools or grown-ups. That's how children are now, now that they *know:* their mistrust is oppressive but intermittent. They listen, and then play for a bit, then look at us without saying anything, and return to their game. We are still giving her news of her *papa*, in the Maquis, and she listens with delight at first, and then looks rather thoughtful. Or am I imagining it? Does she really believe the stories we tell her? Or is it rather that she wants to believe them? That is the unnerving mystery of children. For them what matters is the here and now, the Gestapo is just a vague word, but fear is real, and Sylvio can pin her latent anxiety onto a thing, a person, a bogey-man, an unkind friend. . . She worries about the pointed questions asked at the school I sent her to, about her father's job, and now about his absence. She often says strange things, which she then then immediately forgets, for example 'Do you know, Maman, I dreamt that they were putting Zabeth[49] in a big box

49 Her two-year-old cousin.

at the station, and on it someone had written "Deportation" in big letters. What does that mean?' Another time, right in the middle of the station at Aix-les-Bains, where we were making another hasty departure, amidst all the confusion, she asked loudly, 'Maman, what are we called now?' And one morning, in the street, when a stranger asked her how old she was, she turned to me and asked anxiously, 'How old am I, Maman?' Then last autumn, when my mother was still living at her flat in the Avenue Henri-Martin, men from the Gestapo suddenly appeared. Sylvio pretended to be asleep under the sheets. She has never talked about it. What do our children really know about *our* fear? So close to it and yet so removed, often they seem to leave us, to abandon the adult world in which time moves on, to live in their own eternal present.

What a sad afternoon! The oppressive feeling didn't lift for a single second. Even my wonderful friend Madeleine with her glorious mop of blonde hair failed to brighten my gloom. Two or three others arrived. Someone said how charming they found Josée de Chambrun.[50] What a strangely dated, almost tragic ring that sentence has. At one point, while we were discussing how the Germans had stolen our furniture, a woman in a pink hat announced, 'We lost a lot of things too! Don't imagine we got everything back. Why, when we all left Paris, I lost three silk slips!'

---

50 The daughter of Pierre Laval, married to René de Chambrun.

16TH AUGUST

One young man has got out of Fresnes prison. This morning he went to see Mme Capiot,[51] (where César, Félix and Fil de Fer hid) with news of André, César and the others. It seems that one of them is in a very bad way, I don't know if it's Ernest or Cachoud. César and André are all right. This young man was in the next cell to André and said he'd been interrogated three times. My God, I'm shaking. But it seems he's all right. He sent me lots of messages; he's even asked for his warm anorak. (I've no idea where it is now.) He's in good spirits, thank God. According to Nadine, the lad who got out of prison is a black marketeer from the Milice. It all sounds bizarre. He's meant to be coming to see me tomorrow, and he'll try and get some parcels to them.

17TH AUGUST, LATE

This evening I had dinner with Gigi G, who was imprisoned in Drancy for a few months. While she was there, she worked as a nurse, and looked after my mother-in-law, who arrived there ill, with poor eighty year-old *grandmère*. They were both in a pitiful state; their flimsy shoes tattered and their stockings in shreds; and utterly exhausted.

My mother-in-law spent the whole time lying in the camp sick-bay. Gigi G was deported in the same convoy as my parents-in-law, at the end of November. But she managed to

51 The *concierge* at the Rue de la Tour, who hid César and his friends.

make a miraculous escape, alone, with no help, just her own courage, and careful planning, a pile of pullovers to soften the fall when she jumped, and a torch, which saved her life. She is still very ill.

The cycle ride from the Porte Champeret to the Place de la Porte-d'Auteuil, where she lives, was strange – exhausting, but I found the strength somewhere, that reserve of nervous energy which seems always about to run out but somehow goes on renewing itself. It was dusk and very beautiful, and as I rode along the edge of the Bois de Boulogne my thoughts went back to the time when I lived nearby, to places which were part of my past and now seem no more than absurd figments of my imagination that no longer exist other than for me. I pedalled back into my childhood, into my youth, a period which no longer means anything to anyone else. In the soft August warmth, as the battle raged this evening, I returned once again to my process of self-examination, watching my shaking nerves, my physical and mental tiredness, reflecting on the exhausting struggle in which I am engaged, and on my hidden wounds, which will not heal.

And I think to myself that I am coping in a way, but only just. It seems to me that events carry us along only so far, that they can shoulder us for a while; they provide us with some external, impersonal strength, but before long we are thrown back on our own resources, left to bear the burden, abandoned each to our true self, the one that we drag around always, disguised, made-up, sometimes naked, and bearing the scars of old wounds. This chameleon self wears worldly colours that nothing can change – not even the greatest of undeserved sorrows.

At the Porte Maillot, where the Bois de Boulogne begins, the trees are still lush and green but here and there are the first golden tones of approaching autumn; the fairground stalls are still there, in the shade of the tall trees, beside the circus; for me nothing has really changed, apart from the whine of passing German lorries breaking the summer silence. It's still the same magical Bois de Boulogne as before; as a child in Paris this was my countryside, and my forest. I can still see myself as a little girl, playing here during the '14–18 war, in the Allée des Fortifications which I am cycling along this evening; I see that small child hurtling with her friends down the slopes of the old 1870 defences to play down at the bottom, in the wide ditches full of scrub and thorn bushes, broken bottles and litter, as well as wonderful spring flowers peeping up here and there from beneath the piles of dead leaves. We used to run along the slopes, until we were out of breath – I was always at the back – deaf to our governesses' horrified cries, which receded into the distance as, with pounding hearts, we raced towards some new adventure. I would lag behind, pale and peaky, excited by the race, and tearful at the same time, without really understanding why. There was so much emotion in the air then, signs of the war were everywhere: women in mourning, crêpe veils, whispers, and words reaching down to us from the mouths of grown-ups, who seemed so remote to us, mysterious, important words radiant with the glory of France, names like Maréchal Joffre, the Marne, Foch, Verdun, the Chemin des Dames. How close that child seems to me now: out of breath, slightly lost, always looking for somewhere to run to, for a large hiding

place, a big boat hung with pennants, a huge space, a cathedral, an entire homeland, somewhere big enough to contain all her love, to hold her anxious heart that beat too fast, and was waiting for someone, even then. Perhaps an absent father. How similar that child was to the woman I am now, the child and the woman bound one to the other over the years, fused together, becoming eventually the person I am now, this evening, as the battle continues, lost, out of breath, alone, pedalling and pedalling, waiting for news of someone she loves.

I can still see those little girls, the little Kahn girls, the Weils, the Dreyfuses (from the Jewish[52] community of businessmen, bankers and stock-brokers who lived in the XVIe arondissement) who, like me, used to play in the Allée des Fortifications, well brought-up and well-dressed, like me, in clothes from Jones in the Avenue Victor-Hugo, in tailored coats, gloves and hats, accompanied by immaculate, severe and snobbish English governesses, wearing starched white collars, carrying our snacks in their bags, along with Thermos flasks and folding stools, all the clumsy paraphernalia of the well-to-do. Little girls from smart Paris addresses, who fondly imagined that their families had always lived there, poor innocents, and that they would be there forever. I can picture all the other little girls too, Morel, Verne, Lefort, and many more. Childhood friends, whose young faces are flashing

---

52 J M-A in fact used the word *Israélite* when speaking of Jews whose families had lived in France for several generations – French Jews. The term *juif* was used for those Jews who had arrived in France, mainly from Eastern Europe, during the 1920s and 30s – foreign Jews.

before me this evening, faces from a time long gone now, when we played, and ran about together, with no thought for surnames, or noses, families, or race, interested only in our friendships and the fun we had together.

Later on I was oddly drawn, although I didn't realise it at the time, towards the 'others', alluring angels, happy-go-lucky demons, constantly bubbling over with laughter. Did I have a repressed longing to be like them, to have their confidence, their charm, their easy gaiety, the fruits of generations of security, of happy extended families, holidays in old family houses, in remote and sleepy countryside, filled with grape-picking and harvesting and hunting, with strange family rituals, and laughter? How I loved the stories of their catechism classes, which made them giggle so much, their accounts of secret meetings with boys after Mass on Sundays; I was even fascinated by their spiritual crises, their sudden fervent upsurges of faith. I feel a certain nostalgia for them, for the 'others', for their faces, for the places they came from. Why? Do we, children of Israel, but no longer Jews, have an unassuaged yearning to belong, a longing which burns sometimes in the heart of a Jewish child?

Or did it mean nothing? Pure chance perhaps? Simply that, long ago, in the Bois de Boulogne, some of the little girls who lived nearby, in the Avenue Henri-Martin, or the Avenue Victor Hugo, or the Rue de la Faisanderie, were fun, and wild, lively as mountain streams, and swift as boys, young Amazons, or voluptuous and treacherous as cats. There was Denise, who was like a bird, a child of Greek antiquity, and full of charm, if a little unkind. She had very short spiky black hair, like dark feathers around her mocking wide eyes. Jacqueline, blonde

and beautiful – the most beautiful of them all – with long legs, a young proud Atalanta who ran wild races, had violet eyes, and intense passions. And Raymonde, who was dark and sensuous, in a way that showed already in her hazel eyes, deceptively gentle and very obstinate – she is still my friend now, in these tough times; and Marie-Rose, energetic and high-spirited, a real tomboy and now a very dear friend.

Was there something different about us, the little Jewish girls? I can no longer tell. Were we perhaps a little more anxious, were our eyes darker, were our friendships more intense, were we more conventional at home? Of course we were all equally French – if in a different way – whether we were little *Israélites* from old established families, or newly arrived from other countries – all passionately French. What fatal path, what devastating shortcut through the thickets of history, intersecting with their ancestral destiny, had led some of these well brought-up little girls from the Avenue du Bois, from the Allée des Fortifications, to Auschwitz?

Most of us went to the same elementary school, at that period when our whole lives stretched ahead of us, and afterwards we all went to the Collège Fénelon in the Rue de la Pompe (what a grim street!); it was a dark and dusty building, painted chocolate brown inside, like all the best secular secondary schools of the period, and very fashionable. The First World War had been over for years, but headmistresses still held to late-nineteenth century *revanchist*[53] principles.

---

53 **A** term which originated in France following the Franco-Prussian War (1870–71) among nationalists bent on revenge and determined to reclaim the lost territories of Alsace-Lorraine.

They were patriotic and highly moral. Make-up was frowned upon, fraternising with boys forbidden. But our school was directly opposite the huge ugly building of the Lycée Janson, and during Latin lessons the girls' thoughts would wander to the handsome, spotty, sixth-formers who had floppy hair and wore fashionably baggy trousers in an attempt to look like Bright Young Things. All flown now, those classroom years of my lonely childhood, when I worked furiously, willingly, late into the night. What dreams filled my young head! The intoxicating thrill of learning; the fire of adolescence, the first and the finest, that life quenches so effectively, little by little; the passion for beauty; all the emotion inspired in young hearts by the lives of great men; the conflict between love and duty that we discovered in Corneille; such a frenzy for books that they all merged into one; a sense of ambition which was both vague and delicious. And, of course, before long, first love.

We would walk home together, my friends and I, in little groups, which varied from day to day; in our final years at school we would talk endlessly about poetry, and love, and ourselves – mostly about ourselves – as we went along the featureless streets of Passy, pausing in the quiet squares, then continuing down the handsome avenues to our houses, where cups of hot tea would be waiting, however late we were. It was a warm and sheltered life, a spoilt child's life, a pampered life which produces children who never grow up, one which felt to us both oppressive and quite natural: it demanded obedience, and it could be stifling. At that time paternal authority was absolute and repressive. But what a fine shelter our houses provided. I can remember our own, so bright and glittering

and when there was a party the scent of flowers and fine wine and ringing with voices, whereas normally it was calm and quiet, thickly carpeted, and immaculately tidy; to me my father's house seemed like a fortress, a little Versailles, a battleship anchored in Paris, far away from the rough waters of ancestral anxiety. Even our schoolwork protected us. We loved it and we felt so comfortable at school, secure in the confines of the exam syllabus and the annual prize-giving, sheltered by them from the perils of life outside. We were safe in the bedrooms of our girlhood, and in our mothers' drawing rooms. Rather more distant was the shelter of our fathers' offices: mythical, powerful, inaccessible offices in the heart of Paris, dusty places, irresistibly alluring, the unknown source of the great river of Big Business! How far removed we were from real life, even in the lecture rooms of the Sorbonne, in the libraries, in the English Department, even in suburban health clinics (to which our old governesses continued to accompany us, if only in spirit). The walls which protected us then seemed impregnable. But now those homes have crumbled away, they shelter other people, the old voices are silenced, our fathers' offices have been reduced to ashes, pathetic vestiges of illusory power; and they themselves have been condemned and torn from us, condemned to a life of wandering, or condemned to death, those colossi, demi-gods, the fathers who held up the pillars of our temples. The destiny of Israel . . . And here we are, poor homeless children, exposed, shivering and fighting bare-knuckled, alone from now on.

I go past Boulevard Lannes, bathed in sweat, pedalling furiously – I've lost so much weight these past weeks I must

be barely recognisable. Here is the S's house. I can still picture the ball they had for their daughter's eighteenth birthday. It seems quite unreal. How beautiful she looked, with her fine Mediterranean features, her long straight neck, high clear forehead and wide almond eyes, like a young Cretan, and already breaking the hearts of two young students, and so many others.

I was wearing a green dress that evening, which you liked. I was seventeen. Do you remember, André? I was so worried that you wouldn't think me beautiful! Because of all the other girls there. Did we talk of love that evening? Like a lot of young intellectuals, you didn't dance very well: your dancing was straightforward, rather shy and rushed and charming, like the way you spoke, terribly fast because you had so much to say. But I loved your voice, and everything you said. You weren't like anyone else. There was something about you that was vivacious and chivalrous, and slightly Spanish, which you must have inherited from your Sephardic forebears. You had such an open sensitive face, and a kind of innocent romanticism compared to so many of our other dancing partners, who seemed old before their time. Above all you were so unworldly, and you had that lovely sense of irony, light, warm and full of love.

I loved you just as you were: you had no time for the usual Parisian snobbery and obsession with 'career'. Were you still preparing for Ecole Normale[54] or were you already there? We nicknamed you 'Lucien Leuwen'.[55]

54 Institute of higher education established during the French Revolution. It developed into an élite institution for high-achieving French students aiming for careers in the top echelons of the civil service, politics, business and academia.

I can't count the number of dances I went to here, near the Bois de Boulogne. Such foolish memories. It is late now... So many balls, fleeting carnivals, glittering for an evening and fading by morning; those beautiful houses are lived in by others now, but our ghosts are still there, under the trees, in my parents' house, and in the houses of my friends. It is as if the balls of my youth were still going on all around me: I can picture the formal preparations, the sideboards groaning with food set out according to some long-forgotten ritual, waiting for the guests to arrive, the extra waiters, employed for the evening, standing stiffly to attention in their white gloves, the gilded chairs from Belloir,[56] champagne in ice buckets, the fathers casting a patriarchal look around, and us, young girls, with cold hands, hairstyles that didn't suit us and secretly pounding hearts. The first couples would arrive, the plainest friend, the shyest young man, the old schoolmistress, and the disagreeable cousin. I feel I can still hear the bands, the faint sound of fashionable jazz tunes, distant saxophones, the old songs we used to love; I can hear the buzz of voices, the bubbling excitement, all the tender asides by the windows, on the balconies or on the staircase far into the night. It all comes back to me – ghostly processions at never-to-be-repeated parties, at an age when one danced whatever the

55 The eponymous hero of a posthumously published (1894) unfinished novel by Stendhal .The son of a banker, Leuwen is expelled from the *École Polytechnique* because of his idealism. The novel follows his career from the army to government service, via an unhappy affair with a young widow.

56 A Paris business that rented chairs for receptions.

circumstances, even when one thought one's heart was broken. Where are they now, those lost hours, our dancing years? Gone like the foam on the sea, green and white and phosphorescent, and swept under by a single wave. And our dancing partners, where are they? Answer me, my sisters, my friends, you Maryse, you Lise, so close to my heart, answer me, tell me where are the boys of our youth? All those young men who took life as it came, and did the same with the war, what has happened to them? Did they win or lose in the universal shooting gallery, in the absurd fairground of fate? Jacques? Taken prisoner. Philippe, Michel, Maurice all taken prisoner. And you, Pierre, so young, so cheerful, killed in the Ardennes, and Jean-Jacques, lost in 1940 along with his tank, Jean-Pierre killed in a parachute jump, and you Emmanuel, deported. Gone, gone with the wind. Some are with de Gaulle, others are fighting in Italy, and you, André, are at Fresnes with César and the others. And then what, my God, then what?

Meanwhile, in the shadows a sturdy battalion is gathering, a new battalion of elderly women, one former president of the Red Cross, retired army matrons, ministers' ex-mistresses and generals' widows, or women of independent means, their little dogs tucked under their arms, all heading for the local *pâtisseries* in order to eat cream cakes and talk about the war. When all this is over, they will chatter like birds as they eat cake in the *pâtisseries* – post-war cakes. . .

How quiet the Boulevard Suchet is in the fading light. I'm near the end of my journey now, and the end of my *rêveries*. It's curiously peaceful, almost as if a truce had been

declared in this small area of Paris beside the Bois de Boulogne and down to Auteuil. Apart from me there's hardly a soul about.

Now I'm skirting the side of the Place de la Porte d'Auteuil, not far from the little side street where Papa is living (with a former housemaid). It's his fifth or sixth hiding place, a horrid flat, with dusty pink floral wallpaper and skimpy but pretentious taffeta curtains. Still, it's safe. I preferred our old cook's little flat in the Rue Eugène-Sue, in Montmartre, my precarious hiding place last January, where the surfaces were covered in bronze ornaments of fishermen and women, and shells in which you could 'hear the sound of the sea', which had ordinary net curtains at the windows, and an enlarged photograph of her late husband, Monsieur S, over the bed. And at the foot of the dark staircase sat an aged concierge, who 'knew' of course, and nodded her head every time we went past her foul-smelling lodge.

To think that every morning, at exactly the same time, right here in Auteuil, Papa goes out to do his shopping with impeccable punctuality, a hangover from the days when he had an important job: he cuts a dangerously recognisable figure – an elderly Parisian, with something of the retired soldier about him. He is to be seen limping along, leaning on his stick, well-dressed, and wearing his odd elongated hat, which everyone at the Paris Stock Exchange would have recognised in the old days, greeting all the neighbours, chatting to mothers and children; he's smiling and friendly, and his piercing blue eyes don't miss a thing. Seeing this gentle old man walking by wearing his medals, who would guess that

the Gestapo have come looking for him eight times, and that Death has stalked him constantly, at every street corner?

Where does he belong? Is it Lorraine or Paris? He's a Parisian first and foremost of course. And yet . . . Sometimes when I go up in the evening and catch him unexpectedly, bent over his wireless, carefully turning the knobs, the pale evening light falling on his forehead, the face I see is that of an alert old man, wearing a little cap on his head for warmth, and a shawl over his shoulders: there is something atavistic about the image, a figure out of a Rembrandt painting: a Jew, like his father, and his ancestors before him.

Moving from hiding place to hiding place, obstinately refusing to wear the star – 'No, never!' – carrying a barely adequate forged identity card and relying on even less adequate snippets of information from the police, he has survived round-ups, mass arrests and denunciations, muttering all the while through clenched teeth whenever he saw any Germans, 'Scum! Vermin! The Russians will get them'. In four years he has never wavered, never ceased to believe in an English victory. He harbours no illusions about people, nor any bitterness either; he has never asked for help (other than from ex-employees, and then he has paid them) and for hope and reassurance he has relied solely on the BBC evening broadcasts.

Perhaps we were not quite like that, you and I. We had trust in people, trust in life, and at times we were betrayed. We believed in so many things, in happiness, and in friendship. I had even more faith in people than you. I made several approaches to the authorities in Vichy, which turned out to be

not only humiliating but useless. I waited in the corridors of grand hotels, or in toilets converted into sordid ministerial waiting rooms, to be seen, finally, if at all, for a few minutes, by the minister or, more often, by his private secretary. I trusted their kind words, I believed in their good will, in spite of some of the things they insinuated in their polite, icy voices, things like, 'Well, what can I say? There are simply too many of you.'

Yes, I had faith in people. In Paris, I had faith in L, currently so highly regarded by the administration, L who owned a newspaper, whom I used to know well, and whom André had helped in the past. I was certain that he would get me an *ausweis*[57] (I'm still waiting for it), and that he would do something for my young brother-in-law in Drancy. I believed the Italians in Grenoble when they promised to free S, a war orphan arrested for helping the Resistance: I was sure that one of the senior French doctors in Grenoble would provide her with a medical certificate, stating that she was seriously ill. Who didn't I have faith in? I believed. . . what didn't I believe?

A long time ago, right here, in the Avenue de la Porte d'Auteuil, do you remember? In the summer, you often used to come, in the early evening after work, to take me for a walk. I would tear myself away from the deliciously cool house, leave the shady sitting room where thin shafts of sunlight shone through the lowered blinds, leave my white bedroom and my Venetian looking-glass, and the English bookcase and our silver candlesticks. *They* have taken all that now, taken or

---

57 An identity card.

destroyed it. They have wrecked everything. All dead, they killed it, in the same way as they tore up our letters and our photographs, and smashed the toys, smashed our life. But what does it matter? The things we loved were just that, things, beautiful, worldly things, lent to us for an instant. They mean nothing now. All ashes. From now on, O Jacob, we shall dwell in tents, without foundations, or history, secure but collapsible, that will fold away when the wind is against us. What does any of it matter? So long as you come back.

We often used to come past here, on the way to Auteuil to visit friends. Sunset on summer evenings, and people driving in open-topped cars, the air filled with the cheerful sound of peacetime. Then the noise faded away, night fell in the Bois, I leaned my head back and breathed in the scented evening air, and we drove slowly on under the stars.

At the time you were studying for the civil service exams, you had set your heart on it and you were sure of passing, despite hints to the contrary from various quarters.

There were lectures. People to see. Too many people. Endless discussions with friends. Too many friends. Intellectuals, graduates of the École Normale, journalists, prosperous young people from professional backgrounds. We would talk until three or four o'clock in the morning. You all drank lots of whisky, and the conversation meandered from Freud to Marx, to Valéry and Gide, via Montherlant and Malraux, to the aesthetic values of the aristocracy, sceptics, and war writers, and . . .

What did I do all day? I can't remember now. I must have started writing by then, a few short articles, a bit of reporting.

I read, I met friends. I wasted my time, I wasted myself, my youth, my life blood, but I didn't know it then. I used to ride, exceedingly badly; on one occasion I climbed up into a *redoute* dressed as Marie-Antoinette; I went to the theatre to see the Pitoefl[58] and Dullin[59] productions. I took our baby daughter for walks in the Parc Monceau, I went to the health centre in Rueil. And I did some amateur dramatics. I'm rather ashamed of all that now.

> *Idle youth*
> *Enslaved by everything . . .*[60]

We lived, without ever properly learning how, during those brief pre-war, post-university years, just before the first Nazi boots pounded into earshot; slightly guiltily, but ecstatically we took this fragile, marvellous happiness for granted. Of course not everything was perfect. But we enjoyed some unique moments, exquisite friendships, beauty, youth. It's true, we didn't *earn* enough to pay for all that ourselves – even though you worked very hard – and we grew up blind to the harshness and the aggression of the world of business which

---

58 A Russian-born theatre director and producer, Georges Pitoeff (1884–1939) introduced the works of contemporary foreign playwrights to France, notably Shaw, Chekhov and Eugene O'Neill. After his death his wife Ludmilla Pitoeff led the company.

59 Charles Dullin (1885–1949) was a theatre teacher whose students included Antonin Artaud, Jean-Louis Barrault and Marcel Marceau. He played many important stage and screen roles during the 1930s.

60 Rimbaud 'Chanson de la plus haute tour'.

surrounded us; we plucked the fruit before the flowers, and we made a lot of mistakes. We allowed ourselves to be deceived by the mirages of our social class. We – I in particular – loved that Parisian life, the patrician culture, which was, essentially, already part of another era and, worst of all, we failed to foresee the hatred and the horror looming on the horizon, nor were we aware that we were about to be betrayed by a large section of our own social class, a betrayal that would be cold, timorous, and poorly concealed under a veneer of politeness. It was already too late when we began to worry about the German Jews, or the Spanish socialists, when we began to help the refugees who were starting to arrive in droves from every direction. . . We understood too late what was happening. But we lived, worked, tasted everything as fast as we were able; we sampled all that we could of the life that was slipping between our fingers; we danced on volcanoes, we drained our cups, and we loved one another.

How long ago was that? How many years? Centuries?

It's almost dark now. I find the silence that falls on Paris at this time of night very oppressive. Again I am overcome by a sense of mounting dread. One minute I am hot, the next icy cold; I can hardly breathe.

I get to the Place d'Auteuil. Gigi's house is here.

I have come to the end of my journey, I have reached the front of the train, which, when one is travelling by railway, seems to open onto the future, yet it is an illusion, the promise is false. But I have spent a long time in those steamy accordion-like spaces between the carriages, which opened and closed on disjointed periods of my life.

The years press on me tonight, and all the pictures I have of you are in front of my tired eyes, so many images of you at different times: as a young student dressed in light grey that distant spring when we used to meet in the depths of the Jardin de Cluny, or on the island in the Bois de Boulogne, which, with you there, could have been the Alhambra in Granada or the sparkling fountains of Seville. And I see you pale and triumphant, one hot July, after the École Normale examination, having slain your dragons, arriving on the steps of the villa in Deauville; and as my young husband before the war, with your pipes and your books, and then in your army uniform, Chasseur Alpin,[59] of course, like a knight about to go into battle; and finally in the dreadful brown anorak that you've worn the last few winters – a garment designed to protect against the cold, and against fear. Then your steps recede and your outline fades. . . And all my pictures of Paris dance in front of my eyes: the elegant *quartiers* of my youth, the *allées* in the Bois de Boulogne, the Paris of my secret, wandering life in hiding, the beating heart of Paris, all the little streets of Montmartre where I used to walk, alone, living as an outsider, the Rue Caulaincourt, the Place Jules Joffrin, the dreary Rue des Saules, and finally the Rue de Clichy, where I am lodging now, warm and full of life. In my mind I see images of our escapes, and of the round-ups, of your prisons, of meetings at the entrances to métro stations and in cafés, images of Paris, the city in which I have known fear, where I have wept, and where I am waiting for you. . . .

61 Elite mountain infantry of the French army.

Should there be a tomorrow for us, what will it hold? Everything is deathly calm. It is August and my life has stopped. It's a time of waiting, endless waiting: I am empty, reaching out for you with all my being. *'Mi ritrovai per una selva oscura.'*[62]

At Gigi's we hear that several towns in Normandy have been flattened, that most of Caen is burnt to the ground, including all its fine abbeys apart from the Abbaye aux Dames, some of which is still standing. Cherbourg is a heap of ruins, Lisieux a hole in the ground.

They are also saying that before evacuating Caen *they* executed all the prisoners in the city gaol. There was no time to deport them. My God, can this be true?

18TH AUGUST, MORNING

It's been overcast all morning.

I woke up tired in my little attic room. God the sky is heavy! Suzon – my only comfort at present, for dear little Sylvio is a worry – brought me tea in bed as usual. When this is all over, will I still remember my sister's smile, her unfailing support, her immense kindness?

General Leclerc's 2nd Armoured Division entered his home town of Alençon a few days ago, but when is it going to reach Paris? The Germans are putting up a fierce fight from Argentan to Chartres, from Rouen to Dreux. When will our tanks arrive? Is this the price we must pay for our own safety and that of those we love, the destruction of some of the most

---

62 Dante, the second line of *Inferno*: 'I found myself in a dark wood.'

beautiful places in France; must we pay with blood and death and battles?

They still have time to pack up, to empty their offices, to clear out the Hotel Majestic and the *Commissariat aux Questions Juives*. They've had time to shoot the striking railway workers, to empty the prisons, and to deport the prisoners, which they did only yesterday, by train via Pantin.

The Americans are coming, but there's still time for the Nazis to destroy a man, an idea, an entire group of people; as long as *they* are still in control it's the matter of an instant – hundreds of souls can be destroyed in the time it takes to . . .

LATER THAT EVENING

I went back to see Maurice B again. He is still living in the *Cité Universitaire*. He still doesn't know anything about what's happened to the members of our group, at least that's what he says. Perhaps he knows more than he's telling. It's not unusual for him to look as pale as he did this evening, but his blue eyes looked very sombre, despite his best efforts. What a kind friend he is, and so understanding.

As I returned across Paris, an astonishing vision met my eyes. It was nine o'clock in the evening and everyone was outside, standing in the doorways of apartment blocks, on street corners, sitting on benches in the Avenues, waiting outside métro stations. All along the boulevards, along the Boulevard Saint-Michel, the Boulevard Saint-Germain, along the Avenue de l'Opéra, the people of Paris are watching: men, women, children, old and young, watching the Germans leave. It's

their turn to flee now. They're leaving in lorries, in old cars and in trucks, in limousines and on bicycles, all together, piled one on top of another, with no semblance of order or discipline, exhausted and ragged soldiers of a retreating army, carrying eiderdowns, birdcages, iron bedsteads and I don't know what else. Where is the proud German army of 1940? What's happened to the mighty Panzers, that I first saw in Bordeaux? They are fleeing at last. And we are revelling in their flight.

19TH AUGUST

This morning I met Léon A, a cousin of André's, in the Place Saint-Augustin. He assured me that André is at Drancy, with some of the others. He's known this since yesterday evening. He says the whole Fresnes group is now imprisoned in Drancy.

Drancy? Him too. First his parents and his brother and now him. He too has had to endure the horrors of Drancy, like the others, like the rest of his family, forced to share the same tragic fate.

But what is this sinister game of hide-and-seek that is being played out with our prisoners? No sooner do we hear that they are in one place than they've been moved on. The news is changing by the minute. My younger sister has just arrived, saying, 'Drancy is free. It's official. The camp was liberated last night and it's been evacuated today.' So Drancy is empty. My sister and I hug each other, and burst into tears. Our hearts fall silent. Four long years lie at our feet. Suddenly there's nothing left of that place of horrors, the holding pen for Jews, the channel through which countless innocent

people passed, the thought of which has haunted us day and night. It's just a name now, a village, a police barracks.

But alas, that's not the full story. André and the others were not released with all the rest. In fact there's no word of them. Nothing. Nadine telephoned me with the latest information: apparently they are being deported; they were loaded on to a train, the last train the Germans managed to get out, in secret and in defiance of the agreement signed with the Red Cross and the Swedish embassy. The train is carrying fifty hostages, some of them well-known Jews who had been in the camp but were believed to be 'non-deportable': George C and all his family (cousins of the Rothschilds), who were arrested at the eleventh hour, in spite of having friends in high places, Marcel Bloch, the aeronautical engineer (a distant cousin of my mother), and others whose names I don't know yet, and finally, André, César, Ernest (who we had been told was dead), the young 'Wire Man' (he's only seventeen) – in other words, the eight from Fresnes, politicals and *résistants*. The Germans had time enough to do that. Madame de B, whom I saw just now, maintains that the president of the Red Cross is beside himself with rage. But what does his rage amount to, and what's it worth at a time like this? I'm afraid I am utterly sceptical. Apparently the president sent a Red Cross truck to chase the train, and commandeered a car for himself.

Nadine is sure the train will be stopped in France, or that the Maquis will do something, that the FFI[63] will liaise with

63 Following the Allied landings, as France was liberated region by region, local groups of Resistance fighters organised themselves into more

our network and sabotage it. A miraculous rescue mission will be launched to save our boys. The men we love are in that lost train, so it *must* be stopped, mustn't it? How ironic. There will be no more trains snaking across France at night, carrying their caged human cargo towards Upper Silesia, no more sealed trains steaming through the shadows. This is the last one. And you are on it.

There's a curfew this evening. We are shut up in Nana's little sitting room above the soap and oil shop (all of it ersatz even with coupons), where she has entertained so many strange and handsome (too handsome) clients, as well as her elderly female relations. This is the room where they held their secret meetings, and where the young 'chieftain' dished out instructions to the pretty girls. It's stuffy, and we're sewing FFI armbands, with the crackle of machine gun fire in the background from the Place de Clichy and further afield, to entertain us. Windows are their favourite targets.

At around four o'clock this afternoon, my heart heavy, my ears buzzing, and my mind elsewhere, I tried to take Sylvio for a walk: poor little child, she's so pale; she can't bear much more. We went along the Boulevard des Batignolles, towards the Place Pigalle, where the nightclubs are closed and the shutters are down on the cinemas, which still display the conventional smiling face of one-time stars, and there we narrowly

formal units, adopting the name *Forces Françaises de l'Intérieur*. Wearing civilian clothing, identifying themselves only by their armbands, carrying the letters FFI, they provided valuable back-up to the regular French forces. In the last months of the war some FFI members amalgamated with the regular army, while others chose to return to civilian life.

escaped being rounded up. I don't know how, but we managed to slip between the lines of Germans who were jumping down from their vehicles carrying machine guns and surrounding the Place. The crowd suddenly became very nervous and huddled together in tight groups. Then, as if prompted by some signal, the whistle of a bullet perhaps, like wheat being scythed, they made for shelters, courtyard doors or métro stations.

So the battle has begun. The occupying forces have been attacked at various points by members of the Resistance, who have already, we are told, taken over the police headquarters, the Palais Gabriel, the Place de la Concorde, and the Madeleine.

It's very late now, and from our windows the Place de Clichy looks desolate; there's a storm brewing, and a fierce wind is blowing dead leaves around in the darkness.

Where is the train now, the train that's transporting our hostages, which the president of the Red Cross is supposed to be stopping? The last train?[64]

20TH AUGUST

What a mixed-up, frantic day, a day of contrasts – manic bursts of excitement, followed by deep gloom. At breakfast Nana was wearing her shop overall: she was very pale, quite good-looking still, but trembling: it was one of her bad days, and her hair was a mess. After a few harsh words to Edmond, her

---

64 There is a book called *Le Dernier Wagon* (1981) by Jean-François Chaigneau which describes what happened on the last train on 17th August 1944.

husband – 'If you're not happy, you know where the door is' – she turned to the half-open windows, through which we could hear the crack of machine guns. 'Ah, gunpowder!' she exclaimed. 'What a good smell!' We sometimes overlook her 'up, boys and at 'em' side, forgetting that our constant supporter springs from a stubborn line of royalist peasants. But it's petty and mean to criticise her.

We too are aware of the powerful hot acrid smell, but we don't find it thrilling. My sister tidies up Nana's shop a bit, and we pod beans with Edmond (a sweet, kind man, who was badly injured in the First World War, and whom Nana adores) while a huge German tank, with its gun turret turned towards the crowd, manoeuvres gracefully around the Place de Clichy. German cars armed with submachine guns are heading down the Boulevard des Batignolles. They are battling it out for the Citroën garage on the corner of the Rue de Rome.

The sudden emergence of the FFI is astonishing when one thinks about it: they seemed to spring from nowhere, to rise up from underneath the streets in a matter of hours, from pockets of the Resistance, from the bowels of Paris. There are boys of sixteen, maybe twenty, men of forty or more, with that rather wild look that one associates with revolutionaries, Spanish partisans, or the citizen army at Valmy[65] in 1792. Paris street urchins, dressed, or rather dressed up, any old

65 The first major victory of the Revolutionary Wars took place on 20th September 1792 at Valmy. Almost half the army was made up of citizen volunteers. A relatively small battle, against the Prussians, it was nonetheless a very significant victory historically, ensuring the end of the French Monarchy and the establishment of the First Republic.

how – vest and trousers, bare-armed, or in shorts and an old trench-coat – their shirts open, black with smoke, wearing armbands and berets and armed to the teeth – are going around, yelling at passers by: 'They're here! Make yourselves scarce! Beat it!'

And yet it's these teenage 'amateurs', who look so young and so fierce, who are 'holding' the police headquarters, the Hotel de Ville, and apparently the council offices of the VIe, and, in some parts of the city, forcing the Germans to retreat. But the situation is still unclear and very worrying.

Suddenly the crowd in the Place de Clichy begins to grow by the minute: there are some FFI in a car somewhere in the middle addressing the crowd through a megaphone. Impossible to make out what they are saying, but the crowd is applauding. We run over, and are told that the Germans have ceased fire, and are going to negotiate with the FFI. They are leaving Paris today. Instantly people begin to rip up the German street-signs from around the statue of Marshal Moncey in the middle of the Place, breaking them up and stamping on the huge black lettering that we've been forced to look at for the last four years.

At about six o'clock, I go to fetch Sylvio from my parents' apartment in the Rue de Berne to take her for a walk. This noisy battle is tiring and frightening for my little daughter: she's pale and exhausted, and is desperately in need of calm, time in the country and a chance to play. She's had enough of jokes along the lines of 'So, don't you like gunmetal sandwiches then?' We met up with my parents, who were calmly strolling down the Boulevard des Batignolles, like a

typical upper middle-class Parisian couple, as though nothing
untoward had happened to them during the war. But, what a
war they've had! The last time, the eighth, that the Gestapo
called on my mother – who, until March this year could just
about claim to be Italian – it was, as usual, to discover the
whereabouts of my father and my cousin, but this time it was
principally to arrest her if they couldn't get my father. My
mother was at home with Jo, who was calmly in the middle of
a piano lesson – her pupil was wearing the yellow star, as was
my father's secretary, who was there typing flyers. Alerted by
the deliberately loud shouts of the concierge, all three were
able to escape by the service stairs up to the fifth floor, where
some neighbours took them in. A miracle. Yet another. In the
times we are living in, to be alive is always a miracle. And the
man in the light summer suit and the Panama hat is my father,
taking an evening stroll along the boulevard, in his own city,
his Paris, which he is finally able to reclaim after four years of
inactivity, four years of almost total solitude, with the threat
of arrest and death ever-present and without even a newspaper. This is a man who until 1940 would read twenty a day
in the course of his work: during the war he would glance at
one of 'their' papers every morning at the neighbourhood
kiosk, and then, holding it at arm's length, he would hand
it back to his friend the newspaper vendor, saying 'Here,
you can keep your filth'. Maman looks very beautiful this
evening, quite Créole, in a full-skirted dress, with flowers on
a black background, and carrying a parasol – she can still look
astonishingly young. She makes me think of one of Goya's
women, on the ramparts of Seville. There is courage in her

outward frivolity, her determination in spite of everything to keep up a certain style.

They are both walking slowly, and stand out against the crowd, against the greyness and dust of Les Batignolles. They find the revolutionary appearance of the FFI disconcerting, and don't quite trust them. My father says, 'It's all a bit *Frente Popular*.[66] No leader. No uniforms. What times we are living in.' My mother finds our heroes to be rather *mal élevés* (very ill-bred, she said in English).

That's how we are, of course: we are all born naked, but we live and die in our clothes.

At dinner time this evening my mother is waiting for us in the Rue de Berne, sitting at the window with her embroidery, like a woman from another age, as if everything was normal, as if nothing had changed and we were about to have dinner at the villa looking out at the sea and watching the sun set.

It's quite late when we learn suddenly that the situation has changed. The FFI stormed through the city warning people to get back indoors and take down the flags: the Germans were back, negotiation had broken down.

It's totally silent now. There's a storm in the air, and it's pitch black.

66 This was the Popular Front in Spain, created by the agreement of various left-wing parties, which won power in the February 1936 election. Later in 1936 General Franco's right-wing military revolt initiated the Spanish Civil War. In France a similar left-wing Popular Front won the election in May 1936.

VERY LATE

It's at this time of night that I begin to wonder over and over again, 'Where is his train going? Has it passed into the shadows? Is it still in France, the train that should have been stopped by the Resistance, the train in which fate decreed he had to be locked up? Yet another night which is tearing him away from me.

When, quite alone, one digs deep down into one's soul, some strange thoughts emerge – questions about fear and what lies on the other side of fear. Is there an element of choice in the ordeal? How is it possible that one is able, in spite of everything, to bear it, even to accept it? Is there a part of ourselves, a point at which we consent to it, as the price we must pay to cleanse ourselves of the remorse that lies beneath the web of an almost happy life? A kind of penance.

Or is it the simple fact of being alive that I find so astonishing – breathing, eating, being able to go outside – living, betraying. Is it a betrayal to be alive?

Just now when I was walking through the streets, alone, surrounded by people celebrating, I felt a kind of death in my heart. Deep down I had always held onto certain beliefs, naïvely, sceptically, lazily and not always consistently; I had believed in the value of life, and humanity, in spite of everything; I had believed in Justice – a sort of mystical belief, without God. For a long time I have wished that I had a faith, a cause, and suddenly, in the strangest way, I have found both in this terrible war, in these tragic times: first France and then the Jews. Their sorrows were equal and became one in me.

But I didn't know that it is possible for everything, almost everything, to come from one being, one person who lights up everything for us like an invisible but ever-present flame, like the soft warm rays of a summer sun hidden by haze. I had not understood that what I thought of as my Destiny might be my Fate, nor that it was from him alone that I could look for almost all my earthly joy. How foolish I was. Now I know.

21ST AUGUST

There is fighting all round us. Paris is in insurrection mode – resurrection too. Something unfamiliar, dark and febrile has swept through the city, with unexpected ease, a sort of elation, like an old passion rekindled, or an ancient rite revived. The streets and avenues, once so full of people, have emptied in an instant. The silence is total, apart from the whistling sound of SS tanks back-firing and the sound of insurgents' cars as they flash past. A stifling sense of dread hangs over everything, a combination of anticipation, fear and hope. The city is like a feverish giant in whom spasms are followed by periods of prostration and shivering. From out of nowhere, something has surfaced under the skin, in the very soul of the city, which had earlier been mute apart from the sound of gunfire; suddenly something is moving, preparing to unleash itself, something that will not be silenced.

Earlier on my younger sister and I cycled over the Pont Royal, on the way to the Rue de Verneuil, to see Madeleine, who had phoned saying that she needed us. I can't count the number of times we've needed her. 'Let's leave our bikes here,

darling,' said my sister, as we passed the Carousel, 'it doesn't feel right.' They're saying the SS are planning to blow up the bridges, that they are all mined. We rode over anyway. What an extraordinary sight! The city looks strangely empty for this time of the evening. The dense greenery of the Tuileries Gardens in the background, the sombre mass of the Louvre standing guard over the Seine, and, in the foreground, the white bridges, their statues and their arches proud and solitary. This evening Paris looks even more touchingly beautiful – for being vulnerable and threatened. I've never seen my city like this, so bold and so exposed. I love the way she looks now, I love to see her naked face, beneath the disquieting layer of make-up. It suits her. I feel myself trembling suddenly at the thought of what it would be like if the city were to be destroyed.

On our way back we are astonished by how much it looks like a scene of civil war. We are being overtaken by Red Cross vehicles transporting casualties, and already the first flower-covered coffins are appearing. This is street warfare, all the more stressful for being waged in an enclosed city, where the sound of gunfire echoes as if it were in a crater and shakes the houses to their foundations. This has turned into a battle fought by civilians wielding guns, using ambush and cunning, shooting at crossroads, firing virtually from their own houses.

23RD AUGUST

I fell asleep to the sound of gunfire, woke up to the sound of gunfire and breakfasted to the sound of gunfire. Unforgettable. Paris is in a state of frenzy. It must have been like this in 1793

under the Jacobins – I'd never been able to picture it until now. There are three hundred tanks in the city, driving around and around and shooting ceaselessly. The Citroën Garage at Batignolles, seized by the FFI, is still holding out under fire from German tanks. The French, crawling along the ground, on their bellies, are fighting back with machine guns, revolvers, hand grenades. 'If only we had some of the weapons they've got in the Maquis,' sighed one young combatant, a good-looking boy with blue eyes. Fighting continues in the Rue Bonaparte, around the Panthéon, in all those narrow old streets, outside the *Mairie* in the VIe, in 'my' Rue de Seine, in the Rue Mazarine, the Rue Jacob. One of those sudden outbursts that happen in war. Even in the Avenue de Messine, around the Grand Palais, there is fighting.

I'm writing this sitting by the window, at Nana's. Why do I do it? God knows. Is it my escape, like my mother's embroidery? Why have I kept up these scattered notebooks, hiding them all over the place? Some days I've just jotted down a few scribbles, other days I've covered pages, in a futile attempt to record events and how it has felt to live through them, to describe my various hiding places, my journeys, the dark hours of the dawn, the sleepless nights. What has been the point? Whom have I been doing it for?

During a brief lull in the fighting I went to see Suzanne S, in her latest hiding place in the Rue d'Amsterdam. It must be the twentieth, at least, since the beginning of the war: we've followed each other from Bordeaux in 1940, then to Marseille and the Savoie. Her ancestry, her political career, and her beauty made her a prime target for the Gestapo all over France. She

is an astonishing creature, with an extraordinary aura. She seems to float through everything, and come out laughing.

She confirmed that Pétain, Laval and a few high-ranking collaborators have been taken to Germany, supposedly as prisoners. Apparently Pétain absolutely didn't want to leave. No sealed carriages to Auschwitz or Buchenwald for them, in any case! Most definitely not. More likely cars, and plenty of warm clothes. And books? And skis, why not? She also told me that there had been 110,000 applications for German visas (I had thought there might be at most 20,000), and that the General in charge of broadcasting in Paris had refused a lot of them. 'We no longer need you,' were the words he used. Magnificent!

Apparently Sacha Guitry[67] has been arrested. Already! *Sic transit gloria* . . . Things have blown back violently in his face.

Suzanne is rather an 'on-off' friend. I hadn't seen her since André was arrested. She's as beautiful as ever, pale, rather wild, with her famously magnificent hair hidden, for the duration, under a scarf, her wartime headgear. She can conceal her mane of silvery hair but not her amazing, cruel teeth, nor that devastating smile. According to her the war has turned into a blitzkrieg: it won't be long before the Germans are liquidated, and Germany occupied and laid waste. According to her, André will be back soon. 'Very soon, you'll see'.

How soon is 'very soon'?

---

67 Sacha Guitry (1885–1957): Russian born, French stage actor, film actor, director and screen writer, he continued to work on stage and in cinema during the Occupation, and was accused (though later cleared) of collaborating with the Germans. One of the first to be arrested following the Liberation, he was briefly interned at Drancy.

She says all sorts of things. As always, listening to her, I pick up countless snippets of information about who she's met and what she's been doing. As always, I am fascinated, silent and totally passive in the face of the combination of strength, vitality and formidably voluptuous femininity which emanates from her. I find myself swept along by her, caught up in her game, with all its contradictions and inconsistencies; I am bewitched by her sparkling, jet-black eyes, seduced by the charm of that beautiful, slightly mocking voice, by the way she has, when making fun of somebody, of lifting her lip, baring her teeth and adopting a husky, Parisian accent, saying, 'Well, honestly, who does 'e think 'e is?'

She has a way of energising and depressing me at the same time. When I am with her I feel slightly vacant, dazed, as if I was taking someone, or maybe a group of people, to the station to catch a luxury train to a some faraway place in the sun, leaving me behind on the platform, in the fog.

We talked about the people who are contriving to escape scot-free: high-level collaborators, the most important and most highly paid, Déat,[68] de Brinon,[69] Doriot[70] perhaps and

68 Marcel Déat (1894–1955) founded the collaborationist, anti-semitic National Popular Rally, and later, with Jacques Doriot, the *Légion des Volontaires Français* (LVF), a French unit of the Wehrmacht. He was appointed Minister of Labour by Laval in 1944.

69 Fernand de Brinon (1885–1947) was appointed by Laval in 1940 to act as representative of the Vichy regime to the German High Command in Paris. In 1942 he was named Secretary of State.

70 Jacques Doriot (1898–1945): Communist turned fascist, in 1936 he founded the ultra-nationalist *Parti Populaire Français*, later involved in intelligence and sabotage activities for the Germans. He founded the LVF with Déat.

others. Who will pay for what they have done? Some unfortunate pen-pushers of no importance, perhaps the least guilty, or some wretched characters from the Milice, louts who would hand a man over for 2000 francs or a packet of cigarettes. But some of them were no more than sixteen or seventeen. What about the big guys, the ones at the top, the leaders, will anyone be able to touch them? The 'great and the good' are the worst: the very high-ranking civil servant who, from the end of June 1940 onwards, regularly lunched at the Ritz with German officers in uniform, will anyone touch so much as a hair of his head? This was the same man, who a week later, suggested the first anti-Jewish measures to the Germans. Who will dare lay a finger on one or two of our big industrialists? And what about the wordsmiths? I'm thinking of one in particular, the despicable Lucien Rebatet,[71] who directed his venom only at the victims, who takes on only those who are already beaten, tramples only on the dying, and fights only the dead. Who can touch that loud-mouthed lover of Hitler's Germany, the sinister harbinger of German victory, who couldn't wait to lick the boots of the Nazis, who was happy to act as Hitler's agent? For four years he took a wild delight in spewing out his insults, not unskilfully alas, against France, against everyone, saving the worst, of course, for the defenceless and the hounded, for us, the Jews, when our situation was as bad as it could be. My God I can still feel his spittle on my face.

---

71 Author of *Les Décombres* (Ruins), one of the most violently anti-semitic pamphlets to be published.

As for the others, I don't care too much. I just want them to be forgotten. Although I have in mind . . . But how about that upper-class hypocrite, that cruel sophisticate, who, amongst other gems, allowed *Gringoire,* the vile rag that he published in the Unoccupied Zone, to print after the round-up of 16th July 1942:[72] 'Children separated from their mothers – another damn lie.' The blood of others obviously wasn't worth much. Anyway it's for the courts to decide. Does anyone have the right to take revenge?

Suzanne wants to go with me for a roam around the streets, and calls her maid, a beautiful young black girl from Martinique, telling her to 'Get out my dreariest suit'. A tailor-made insurrection outfit. The smart women have put away their fine floral prints, and their hats. It's time for the *sans-culotte* and the *tricoteuse* outfits. That's the latest look.

As I leave Suzanne I am struck that, in spite of all she's been through, she will quickly be swept up in the here and now. Her political friends, her social circle, her own energy, will all ensure that she forgets. Paris will rediscover her. And she will rediscover Paris.

Is it possible that in the vast shipwreck which came close to taking every Jew in France, in spite of everything, her *entourage* should have remained fundamentally the same? Her circle has hardly changed: she didn't make any new friends among those who were suffering and struggling like her. All those foreign Jews for example. far lonelier than us and far poorer. Such easy victims, some of them, pathetic, innocent

72 At the Vel' d'Hiv.

prey, turned over to the executioner, while others, like the young Jewish OJC comrades, fought to the last. Fearless young heroes, hardly more than children, many of whom watched their parents and all their little brothers and sisters being taken away, and whom no one helped, apart from some random neighbour or a concierge who didn't know any deputies, or ministers, or city councillors, or anyone of importance. And, it has to be said, they received precious little help from French Jews. Some of these young people still feel bitter towards France, the country they loved, to which they came with their families, and which abandoned them. I love them just as they are, ill-mannered, awkward, difficult, quick-tempered and fanciful, but often warm-hearted, generous and intelligent: these are people who threw themselves with such reckless courage into the underground war, when it was a hundred times more dangerous for them. They would arrive at Resistance meetings in cafés, or for lunch or dinner, in groups, raring to go, with their girls on their arms – like the others – and their pockets stuffed with revolvers and hand grenades. They were dark-eyed, and sallow-skinned, their accents were foreign, their words unguarded, their assumed names too French, and they were bent on vengeance. Sublime, holy vengeance, the vengeance of God.

Oh yes Suzanne will rediscover Paris and the Parisians. And what about me? After all that has happened, I find myself between two worlds, between two destinies. What kind of Paris awaits me?

23RD AUGUST, 7PM

Chastain, a friend of Nana's who has been in the fighting, suddenly burst into the dining room. He is the hero of Clichy and Batignolles. He is bare-chested and tanned, like a Roman gladiator, with a revolver and grenades hung round his waist, a rifle in his hand, and a black scarf over his cap. He gives an account of his exploits in an accent part colonial, part Parisian working-class. 'We got 'em. There were seven of 'em, Tigers.[73] They were firin' at us non-stop. We were be'ind sandbags. We got the pick-up that couldn't get out, with three Jerries on board. I killed 'em, and three more I took prisoner. I took off their trousers so they couldn't escape. But now the Tigers were clearing off. We got one, threw petrol over it and set it alight. A bloke in the street came up and kissed me!' Chastain, unsurprisingly, isn't a member of any group, he's just a lone fighter, and he's already spotting the profiteers. 'There are blokes driving around now in old Citroën 15s, never been anywhere near a bullet!'

Paris is calmer this evening. People are taking advantage of the fragile ceasefire to get some fresh air. A little old man is walking his dog in the street; children are playing in the dust on the blackened pavements, amongst the broken glass and shell fragments. They are still deathly pale, playing at war, at Landings, at FFI. Two concierges, man and wife, are sitting on kitchen chairs outside their door. He is reading the daily news sheets, which are coming out all at once: *Le Popu*,

73 German heavy tanks.

L'Huma, Le Parisien libéré, all new papers, which, after four years have replaced the French language rags produced by the Germans; she's reading a detective story. They are quietly enjoying the evening air. Paris is getting its breath back.

The Americans are at Arpajon – it's official – and advancing towards Melun, and Versailles. They say that Leclerc's division has reached the Porte d'Orléans. My friend Jacques B phoned to tell me that the Allies are fighting at Massy-Palaiseau; apparently some have got as far as the *Cité Universitaire.* They say . . . apparently . . . Is this really happening? Am I in an enchanted sleep? Will I wake up again in the night? What is this extraordinary dream, the very opposite of the nightmare of 1940?

The city is so on edge. It looks quite different this afternoon. The war is in the streets now, things are changing from minute to minute. Calm gives way to fighting in an instant. One minute people are shopping peaceably or strolling along the street, and children are playing, the next there is the sound of submachine gun fire, the tanks roll in and down come the shutters.

Barricades are going up all over Paris. On whose orders, I don't know. They say the provisional government is trying to prevent the Germans leaving Paris via the north, that the Germans are heading back into Paris with an armoured tanks division commandeered from the Front, or that they intend to stay in Paris and fight the Allies here. Who knows?

What does it matter? We are all fighting now, the only people left inside are the old and the sick: everyone else is in the streets, and the FFI are just the advance guard pointing

the way, leading the insurrection; they are the crack troops holding strategic points against two relentless SS divisions. Barricades are going up at lighting speed. It's as if the people of Paris had been doing nothing else since the days of the Commune in 1871. It's like an epidemic, infecting everyone, whoever they are.

There are old men, women and children working on our barricade in the Rue de Clichy; the florist from the corner has added her dusty carnations and fading roses: even the local prostitutes, with their heavy make-up and bleached hair, have put down their crocodile-skin bags to join in, teetering on their platform soles. They have all formed a chain to pass the cobbles torn up from the streets by the patriots, while they collect sandbags and iron bars and chairs to turn into lethal weapons. The people of Paris have risen up from the depths. Men and women from every social class have been swept up in the frenzy. There are all sorts: strait-laced bourgeois who have finally pitched in, shopkeepers, black marketeers, antique dealers, even some of the most refined interior decorators from the Boulevard Saint-Germain have proved their virility by hurling themselves into the fray ('I absolutely must join the irregulars,' says the blondest of them, with a delicate hand gesture); and there are a few, not many, chic people as well as concierges, students and, doubtless, the sons of collaborators.

The barricade at the Boulevard Saint-Germain is the most popular. One or two of my friends are bustling about providing drinks. Paris is positively bristling with barricades. There's a little one in the Rue de Berne, which doesn't seem

to me to be of much use and which my daughter greatly dislikes, there's one in the Rue de Châteaudun, one at the Avenue des Ternes, one at the Opéra, one at the Boulevard Saint-Michel. They're everywhere. It's all very fine and energetic, but I do rather wonder what purpose they will serve. Never mind. It's marvellous. And I am throwing myself into it with delight.

Nothing can quell the Parisians' fever now. The city is beautiful like this, scarred, and smoking, and chaotic. How Paris has changed in just a matter of days, in a matter of hours!

Blood has been spilt, alas, the blood of Paris, on the streets and on the pavements. Her houses have been damaged, her children hurt. Paris has had her face painted, cannon fire has smudged her eyes a smokey black, bullets have rouged her cheeks, her skin has acquired the pallor of the dying. Death has taken up position at the corner of every street, in the city's beautiful avenues and innocent squares, behind her tall trees, at her café tables and newspaper kiosks, and Death, as always, has struck at random. The soul of Paris, eternally young, is reborn this evening through laughter and tears like liberty itself. Liberty is her vocation, as love is for women: her secret strength, her destiny. For centuries the city has had this tenacious desire to be free. Paris – you are my city, but I didn't really know you. These last, strange days I have rediscovered your fervour, and my own. During this battle, in all its frenzied insurgency – however absurd at times – I have watched you rise again, mystical, city of secrets, more real than during the captive slumber of the Occupation when you were silent, your

beauty damaged more profoundly than in peacetime when frivolous charm or frugal rationality concealed your depths. On the covers of our pre-war exercise books there was a watermark showing the profile of a helmeted warrior, such as you might see on a medal: a similar figure, arm raised and with eyes like fire must always have lain within you, Paris, proud, mad and beautiful.

Just now they are saying in the streets that Leclerc is at Clamart, less than ten kilometres away. Can there be anyone here who is not filled with joy?

Quite suddenly this evening the sky became very beautiful, deep like a Spanish sky, and stained orange by a sunset of indescribable languor. . .

MIDNIGHT

We are all listening to the radio. The signal keeps breaking up, but what we hear is marvellous: a muffled, stuttering voice announcing the arrival of two armoured cars at the Hôtel de Ville. This evening, the 24th August 1944, de Gaulle and Leclerc have reached Paris at last.

They are in Paris, beside the Seine, whose dark waters, on this warm clear night, are shimmering under the stars, whose banks were pounded for so long by enemy boots. They're in Paris after four years!

All the bells of Paris are ringing at once, muffled faintly in the darkness. Nana identifies the little bell of Montmartre for us, the Savoyard, thin and reedy, and the great bell of Notre-Dame, in the distance, and all the others. Why are moments

of great joy also so sad? Why am I crying? The bells of Paris are ringing and ringing. And I am crying for my prisoners, my pale prisoners, out there, on the far side of the world. I am crying for those who have fallen in the last battle, those who died yesterday, this morning, all those who will never know that Paris is free, that France will be free. I am crying for my absent friends, I am crying for my absent husband. He is so far away, where is he going so late in the night? Has he eaten? Has he slept? What's going on in his mind? Does he know that the bells of his city are ringing tonight, and do they know, he and his companions, do they know the wonderful news, that Paris is free? Do they know that they *have* to live, because the world is about to be free?

It's late now, and I'm still up. The others have gone to bed, but I can't sleep. What is happening is so important, the world, our whole lives have been turned upside down while the universe and the stars remain sublimely indifferent. I am looking up at the vastness of the sky, turning above me.

For a moment, Fate swept me up in her wake, a poor little actor on an oversized stage, in a vast theatre. I played my part, my ancestral role, I was one of the hunted. For an instant History carried me on her wings, and lent me her light, and my soul beat to the rhythm of Paris; I was one with Paris, and the fibres of my being pulsated with those of my race, with whom they are forever enmeshed. But it's nearly over. The end is coming, the curtain is about to fall. Soon I will be thrown back on my own destiny, I must return to my own personal anguish, to my own life, my little life, inward-looking and enclosed like all lives.

I have forgotten you, God of my fathers, you who never forget; my God, if it is your will, you would give me back my life's companion, you would lend him to me again to take life's path together, just as he is, with his warmth and all his faults. I will slough off my proud, rebellious, demanding self, I will give up my personal ambition and step into the shadows, I will make any sacrifice to have him here. So that we might start again, and live a life of new beginnings, of risks and worries, so that we might rediscover the wonder of being alive, of being together, have hope, and test the limits of human happiness.

25TH AUGUST

No one slept. Early this morning, out of habit, I listened for the sound of gunfire, but all I could hear coming from the courtyard was the sound of birdsong, dogs barking, a shutter banging, something grating on the cobbles, nothing but village sounds in the city. One might almost have been in the countryside.

The weather is now quite extraordinary. Summer has burst like a ripe fruit, even more beautiful for having come so late.

Here Nana's network is in a state of frenzy. People are going up and down in the back of the shop, all yesterday's young *résistance* workers dizzy with delight at being able to emerge from the shadows, enjoying the thrill of being out in the middle of the day: it's as if they were on holiday. Their young chief, a tall, handsome chap of about thirty, is a terrific hit, and the radiant girls, with their hair newly done and their

faces freshly made up, have invaded the shop and the flat: it's in turmoil. Nana is in her Sunday best, a black silk dress and flowery hat and her smartest shoes, and she's laid out a feast, food that she'd been saving, pâtés and preserves. She throws open her cupboards and throws open her heart. But there is still fighting at the Trocadéro, at La Muette, and around the École Militaire, and there's a major battle going on at the Pont de Sèvres between American and German tanks.

By 3 o'clock it's all over. The Armistice has been declared and this time it's for real. The street is full of people. I see Chastain, the hero of Batignolles, go by wearing a sports vest, white spats and a red fez, followed by a vast crowd. The Clichy sun has given him a tan! His pregnant wife was devotedly carrying his helmets, his weapons and all the rest of his accoutrements. Cars are driving in every direction packed with FFI guys.

At around 6 I powdered my face and put on some lipstick and a clean dress and got out my old wartime bike and rode through the streets, along the Rue de Clichy, the Rue de la Trinité, and the Rue Saint-Lazare. Then I went back towards the Faubourg Saint-Honoré to see what was going on. I went to see Jacques B who lives there. Suddenly there is a lightheartedness over the whole city, people are singing, running, everyone is on the streets, parties are being planned, there will be dancing this evening on every street corner. The flags are out, flags made out of scraps of material, hastily dyed and roughly stitched. French *tricolores* and allied flags are hanging from the windows, and wallpaper banners stretch across the streets from house to house, swaying in the air,

glistening against the blue of the sky. These are age-old rituals: since time immemorial towns have hung out bunting to celebrate their victories, and the survivors have danced. And yet so many hearts are aching for someone who is not here.

Now the girls are looking beautiful again, their hair hanging loose, their cheeks rosy and their lips red: happiness is all the make-up they need. Their wide colourful skirts fan out as they run down the Faubourg Saint-Honoré in a kind of impromptu fiesta, joy bursting from every heart. It's a wild day, the light after a long night. I watch from Jacques B's windows as Paris celebrates: the noisy crowds surge around Leclerc's heavy tanks, stationary now and unthreatening, so that women and children climb onto them, all along the old Faubourg, between the print sellers and the fashionable dress shops, past the displays of fine china, lace gloves and golden hair pins.

Why aren't you here, on this unforgettable evening? The sky is so beautiful, why aren't you out there, somewhere in the street, on your bicycle, or here with me on our friend B's balcony, leaning out over the Faubourg, over the whole of Paris? I'm calling you. From the depths of my sorrow and from the depths of my joy, I have never stopped calling you. I'm calling you from a city which is celebrating, a city where the innocent will be able to live, where children will be able to grow up, where those who have done nothing wrong will be able to sleep at night; this is an extraordinary moment of unity, which will not last, but it is a beautiful evening and you would have loved it. You're so far away. I'm calling you as loudly as I have ever called.

25TH AUGUST. MIDNIGHT.

I went out again very late to have dinner in the Rue de Berne with Sylvio and my parents. There are still a few stray bullets flying around, dangerous, treacherous, lethal. But I don't care. I don't care about anything. My joy has suddenly evaporated, and my heart is dead again. I am weary of everything, even of today, which has been too beautiful.

Then, at the corner, turning into their street, I stop pedalling. At the front of the house, on the balcony of their dreary flat, something moved. I think I see my younger sister. She is leaning right over the balcony, waiting for me, and signalling, wildly signalling. She's calling me! My heart is beating so fast I can hardly move, my legs turn to jelly. I think they might collapse under me. If she's calling, it must mean . . . And now I hear her voice. Am I hearing properly? 'We've got news! Hurry! Come quickly! André's escaped.' I stop. My body freezes. I can't move. Will I ever move again? She runs down to me, with my little girl, whose face, looking quite grown-up, is glowing with excitement. Suddenly I understand. I begin to run, I'm flying, I believe her. One of the group telephoned, I don't know when or how. They escaped; they sawed through the bars, and some of them jumped from the moving train, a few nights ago. They managed to jump from the last train. It was raining. The rain gave them cover, it saved them. They have walked all the way from Saint-Quentin. César's legs are very painful, and André is waiting for him. But they're not far from Paris, they're on their way. They will be here tomorrow.

PHOTOGRAPHS BY
THÉRÈSE BONNEY

PUBLISHER'S NOTE

Thérèse Bonney (1894–1978) was a war correspondent who travelled throughout western Europe – France, Spain, England, Sweden and Finland – taking photographs of the children devastated by the conflict; in 1943 these were published in her book *Europe's Children 1939–43*. The photographs had minimal captions eg. the first one, labeled France, is 'Anywhere, everywhere', the second, labeled Spain, is 'In wind and rain they beg – they search for food' and so on. The photographs are reproduced courtesy of The Bancroft Library, University of California at Berkeley.

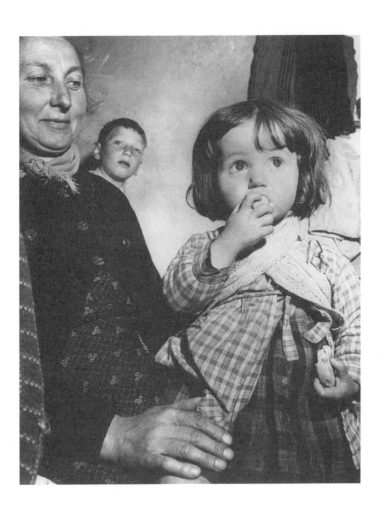

PART II
FROM TRAGIC TIMES
TO DIFFICULT TIMES

PART II
FROM TRAGIC TIMES
TO DIFFICULT TIMES

These articles first appeared in the *Bulletin du service central des déportés israélites*. They have been chosen to illustrate the periods of waiting, followed by hope, and finally the realisation of the full horror. They are preceded by the introduction written by Jacqueline Mesnil-Amar for the 1957 publication of this book by Les Editions de Minuit.

INTRODUCTION

On 19th August we heard that Drancy had been liberated.

The battle for Paris had begun. We were walking on air.

Then, one evening [on 24th August] at around 5 o'clock the gunfire stopped. That night at midnight all the bells began to ring at once, quietly at first, in the soft shadows, ringing for freedom, for the right to live. After four years the bells were ringing for us all, for the suffering, for the outcasts and for those on the run, for the dead, for our fellow

Frenchmen, for our fellow Jews, for our fellow human beings. Our hearts were torn between joy and sorrow at the thought of those who would never know, who would never experience, the beauty of this strange night, which seemed to stretch blindly towards the dawn, bearing the promise of a new day.

The following morning brought the return of five or six men from our group who had been caught by the Gestapo in the 18th July trap.

They had hurried through the celebrating crowds to meet us and arrived looking like men miraculously brought back to life; they were wild, hungry, filthy and ruddy-faced, reminding one of lads escaped from the siege of Barcelona. They were alive, wonderfully alive: their clothes were torn, they had no shirts, and their shoes were in shreds and they were intoxicated by everything they saw – the flags, the flowers, the soldiers, the girls in their thin brightly-coloured summer dresses, all flooding towards the Champs-Élysées where de Gaulle was expected, all caught up in the crazy, ecstatic whirlwind of liberated Paris.

On the fourth night of their endless journey, they had managed to saw through the bars of the roof-light and about ten of them had jumped from the deportation train[74] taking them to Germany. They had escaped somewhere north of Saint-Quentin, between midnight and one o'clock in the morning, in the pouring rain – it was the rain that saved them – on the 21st August. They spread out in groups of two or three and walked fifty kilometers in four days without money

74 cf. fn. 64

or papers, their pockets full of nails (for puncturing German tyres). It was a perilous journey: the country was still at war, criss-crossed by retreating enemy troops, but by some miracle they reached Paris the very morning it was liberated.

26TH AUGUST 1944

There are moments when our lives seem to have been touched by the hand of God. There is fate in joy, just as there is in sorrow. The sun was shining and Paris was living through one of those searing days of revolution that are so much part of its history, days which belong to the crowd. The warmth of the sun infused our own private joy: it was a regeneration, a triumph over fate, however undeserved, a miraculous rebirth. For in this sudden moment of harmony, dazzling and so brief, we were at one with the world. We were free. It had happened. We were free and we were alive.

That day, for the first time in four years, we were at last like other people: we were able to laugh in the faces of the Milice about our false papers, burn our yellow stars or put them away in a box, we could say our names out loud, give our real names on the telephone, in the streets, in shops and in restaurants; we were no longer 'foreigners', outsiders, keeping to the shadows in our own city, no longer fugitives hunted down from house to house, from attic to attic. Our identities had been given back to us: we were part of society again, part of France . . . part of the war. Now at last we were like everyone else and there was just one war, the real war. Everything was simple again, so easy, we could face anything, now that we all

shared a common fate: it was intoxicating. We could bask in a deep, wonderful harmony. We were *reconciled*.

But that sort of joy is short-lived. It was a strange autumn. We had nothing: no light, no bread, no butter, in fact almost nothing (which didn't stop us inviting our young American liberators to dinner). It was a thrilling time, but little by little we each had to rediscover our old selves, the petty and demanding selves from which we had enjoyed a break, which we had forgotten during our terrible, tragic 'holiday', and we had to discover how to live with this 'other'. We became ourselves again. Then all the old anxieties returned. Paris was free, but the world was still at war. Some friends were safe but even now others were on their way to Germany and beyond, lots of others, the weakest and the oldest. And what had happened to those who had been deported first, in the early days of the war, our grandparents and parents, our friends and relations, who had been gone for so long, since the end of 1941, '42, '43, '44?

All sorts of wild rumours flew around and we seized on them immediately. People said that some of the trains carrying deportees had stopped at Strasbourg, and that the sick had been held there; they said that the UGIF[75] had received 1200 postcards, that the families had recognised the handwriting, and that no one was complaining, saying only that the work was hard but that everything was fine: someone had apparently asked for a pair of shoes. One young woman was said to have received a letter from her husband, who had been

75 *Union Général des Israélites de France.*

deported in December 1941, saying that he was working as a chemist in a factory. We heard that others were working as cashiers, or doing office work, while the strongest were working on the land or in the mines. It was very hard, of course, but there was reason to hope that we would see them again. People thought that perhaps the old were being kept in some sort of hospital. Children, they said, had been spread about the countryside, hidden in farms – but they would be found. There was no doubt, they would be found. . .

The truth was that nobody knew anything. Not a single postcard had been received, not a single escapee had been sighted. The French Red Cross knew nothing, having barely gone beyond their limited remit; the Swiss Red Cross *said* nothing other than to convey a bizarre optimism based on reports from the show camp at Theresienstadt which had a Town Hall, a Casino . . . dances for the inmates, everything, in short, but a post office, and which was nothing but a puppet camp, set up solely to satisfy the curiosity of the Red Cross representatives, a curiosity which, as it turned out, they did not have.

Quite soon we realised that, whatever the cost, we were going to have to break down this wall of silence. Other far more sinister rumours were beginning to circulate in post-Liberation Paris, we were hearing terrible reports on the BBC about Ravensbrück and Auschwitz; a Polish officer had published an account of the final hours of the Warsaw ghetto, a sort of hideous torch was beginning to shed its light over central Europe. Our hearts were filled with a new despair.

After three weeks the men of our group who had escaped decided to set up a centralised service to collate everything that could be found out about our friends and about all Jewish deportees and their families, since they, alas, represented the majority. The *Service Central des Déportés Israélites* was formed in September, with the dual aim of working both with the Ministry for Deportees and the Allied armies to pursue every conceivable line of research, and to publish their findings.

We produced a monthly bulletin summarising our activities, our searches and the information we had collected, grim evidence that was beginning to come in from all sides, in unpublished reports from Switzerland, Belgium and Poland. It recorded our fears, our mistakes, and the hopes which, confronted by the truth, were crumbling one after another; and, until September 1945, charted our rapidly dwindling level of confidence and its final, irreversible collapse. We tried to convey as fully as we could the extent of our shock, of our pain, and of our fury in the face of the indifference shown by the rest of the world then and now. The full history of the camps is known the world over nowadays: any number of books have been written about them, classics, one might say, since we have become so disturbingly used to the horror; but the first details of the atrocities were recorded in these pages, little by little, sentence by sentence, from the mouths of the survivors themselves. After 8th May 1945 they began to arrive at our offices in the Hotel Lutétia, in small groups, one after another, still in their striped prison uniform, and with shaved heads: speaking in monotones and with few hand gestures

they gave a stark account of what had been happening, only eight hundred kilometres from Paris; what they described was the absolute and total obverse of what we think of as civilisation.

'Tell them, just tell them,' they repeated over and over again. And then, having said what they had to say, they went out into the streets, waiting for a time when they might become like other people again and merge into the crowd around them.

And we did tell their story. We told it for all those who didn't know it . . . And we told it for all those who have forgotten. And we collected some of these articles for all those who will forget in the future.

15TH NOVEMBER 1944
WE ARE ALL RESPONSIBLE

These past weeks we have been reading horrifying things. With an almost desperate urgency, every one of us has fallen on the accounts that have been coming out. In the daily newspapers or in private documents we have read about the pogrom at Tarnow, and the massacres at Birkenau; in the British periodical *Twentieth Century* we read an account of the extended horror of the Warsaw ghetto, already a matter of historical record, in which the Germans held 1,800,000 Jews in atrocious conditions, requiring, from 1942 onwards, that a regular quota be taken each day to the station to be dispatched to the extermination camp at Treblinka: a thousand at first, then three thousand, then seven thousand, then ten thousand

– ten thousand people a day to Treblinka, in cattle trucks
with quicklime for latrines. Then there was the account of
the treatment meted out by the Germans to their Russian
prisoners, and particularly Russian Jews; or 'Memories from
the House of the Dead', written by a Polish officer about
some of the camps in Upper Silesia, where at one time the SS
found it entertaining to wake the poor wretches who were
working sixteen hours a day and force them to do a little
'PE' in the middle of the night or to make the Jews who had
been condemned to the gas chamber stand for hours in a
'waiting room' carrying soap and a towel as if for a shower;
and the Belgian report published in September 1945 describ-
ing 'the wagon of death', in which 145 people (it had been
made to hold no more than 50) suffocated after three hours,
piled one on another, without even the smallest chink of light
or air.

A HAILSTORM OF ATROCITIES

Every day we hear of a new one, worse than the last; every day
our hopes fade a little more; but, like Oedipus on his fateful
search for his father's killer in Thebes, we carry on, driven by
our unshakeable conviction that the tragedy has indeed
occurred, and we must carry on because we need to know the
truth.

But, in all honesty, if each and every one of us had not had
someone dear to them in German hands, would we be so
eager for knowledge, would we be so overwhelmed by what we
are hearing, so driven by our almost holy rage?

In his preface to 'Memories from the House of the Dead' the writer twice calls on the conscience of the civilised world which, he says, 'with serene indifference and in almost total silence allowed a crime to take place, which, in cruelty and scale, exceeds anything that men could previously have imagined.'

The conscience of the civilised world – what is that? What does it mean? Is there irony in the words? Perhaps not, or, if there is, we are all accountable. Perhaps we should not always lay the blame elsewhere, on others – Général de Gaulle, Anthony Eden, the Allied Armies, President Roosevelt. It's too easy. The conscience of the civilised world belongs to everyone, it's your conscience and mine. We are all responsible. Human beings are responsible for one another and they must be answerable not only for the things they have done but also for the things they have not done, not only for the things they have thought about but also for those they have failed to think about. History is made up of an infinite series of links, a whole network of responsibilities. When, in the old days, the Polish Cossacks carried out a pogrom in the ghetto in Minsk, the German Jews said, 'They're only Polacks', and so no one feared for the future and Hitler's rise was met with too little resistance, too little horror. Which is why, in 1933, French Jews felt perfectly safe in what they thought of as their country, their houses, with their government, why they remained blind and deaf to the suffering of German Jews: 'It couldn't happen here, not in France, not in our country,' they said, and left the fifth columnists to do their worst. In 1940 and 1941, after the first *Statuts des Juifs* were passed, we, the French Jews, began

frantically looking back into our family history, counting the centuries we had been in France, counting the generations, counting the medals, counting our war-dead. 'These measures are for foreign Jews,' we said, and that is why we found ourselves thrown into the same camps, just as alone, just as naked, just as abandoned as the poorest, most wretched Pole. Neither the then Minister of Justice, nor the Council of State, nor one single official lifted a finger to save any of their compatriots covered by the Statutes, thus effectively handing them over to the Nazis; they denaturalised the foreign Jews and denationalised the others (those who were French by birth), refusing to change a single name, or provide a fresh identity to a single person, on the grounds that they were 'only Jews, after all'. And so, not because of the rigid law of cause and effect, but because of the mysterious law of nature by which injustice and barbarity are contagious, the law which causes injustice and barbarity to spread exponentially, the Germans turned their fire on other targets. The old rage was reignited in all its fury and spread freely all over France, against the martyrs of the Limousin, of the Ain, of the Vercors, killed with pitchforks, tipped from a truck into quarries, or buried alive . . .

Everything is connected. Humanity is bound together. All crimes are collective. Desperately concerned as we are for our own deportees over there, whose fate haunts our days and nights, we must never forget the horror of every torched house, the tragedy of every hostage shot, or the fear of every naked victim shivering in the cold.

In the words of the great poet John Donne, '. . . never send to know/ For whom the bell tolls/It tolls for thee.'

15TH DECEMBER 1944
FOR THEM

It is for the deportees that we must work now, day and night; we must think about them day and night; all our attention, all our efforts and all our love must be directed towards those whose fate by some inexplicable miracle, by some oversight of Destiny, we have been spared.

We were not forced to leave, we who are working here, we are the Jews who stayed behind: we were not led out at dawn from Drancy Block 4 (the one set aside for prisoners awaiting deportation) after nights on the ground with no blankets; we were not loaded into lorries and taken to the station at Bobigny; we were not kicked into cattle trucks, not thrown onto the floor surrounded by crying babies, by the old and the sick and the mad . . . and the dying, all covered in filth, with buckets for latrines which could not be emptied, we did not have to travel with them in stinking suffocating carriages; we were not on the trains with our brothers and sisters and parents, hundreds of trains, freezing in winter, stifling in summer. We weren't the ones, anguished and facing death, forced to leave for the flat lands of Central Europe from which none have yet returned.

It's four months since Paris was liberated and we shall live again. We are living again. One day, if we are able, we will live like everyone else. But for now we cannot, and perhaps the reason for that is that we have a duty not to do so. We can't become 'normal' again at a stroke, we can't go up to other people and mingle with them as we used to, we

can't be nice and polite, we can't be the people we were before.

Some very moving articles have appeared in the newspapers, and for the most part they have been deeply sympathetic towards our deportees, if a little harsher towards us non-deportees. *L'Aube* in particular expressed its fear that Jews might be being too impatient in the matter of retrieving their property. Gabriel Marcel,[76] a good friend to the Jews as we know, recently wrote of his dismay at the brusqueness demonstrated by many of us, at our lack of manners, our failure to exercise sufficient self-control, in short 'a shameful degree of resentment'. No doubt he is right, and other writers too, but how could it be otherwise? We are not yet fully human again, not yet properly reintegrated into the human race; something is missing in us, some of our dignity, of our self-awareness; little by little we are finding our way back, working, rediscovering the direction of our lives, re-clothing ourselves in human garb, we are doing it as best we can, numbly, with revulsion or in a state of madness, bitterness, delirium or sorrow. Do our reactions appear inappropriate, are people shocked by them? The fact is that the horrors our families have experienced, the horrors that we have just been spared, which we dream about night after night, the anguish of which is lodged in our bones and in our blood, have no place in normal society: words like tact and politeness no longer mean anything to us, they are quite hollow. For four years we have

76 Gabriel Marcel (1889–1973) was a philosopher, playwright, music critic and Christian existentialist.

lived with these dangers, without glory or justice, and with no help or protection except from the most humble people; we have suffered and died for a destiny we did not choose, we have fought every minute of every day to keep our children, our parents and ourselves from a fate similar to that endured by prisoners in antiquity, who having first had their eyes gouged out, were dragged behind the chariots of Darius, or the Emperor Titus. Day in, day out, from dawn to dusk, we have played this cruel game of hide-and-seek, moving hundreds of times from place to place. Nor must we forget the Jews who fought in the Resistance and faced even greater dangers: is it any surprise that we have forgotten our manners? Perhaps we have saved our souls.

Be that as it may, we are here now to reclaim our share: our share of the human cake, our place at the feast, and at work, which we had succeeded in winning after centuries of being denied them, only to have them taken away again these last four years. This is what we want back, more than our flats, or our shops, our hats or our umbrellas. We want to be able once again to take up our places in life. Perhaps our manner of asking is awkward: are we too bitter, too aggressive, or perhaps too humble? It's not easy for us to strike the right note, not over-anxious to please but not rude, neither too quiet nor too loud. We are not seeking revenge on humanity, but on life, on the brevity of life. You mustn't blame us. The thing is we can't quite be counted among the living, we are barely surviving.

We are the Jews who have been spared, and we have resolved to look after those who were not, to look after 'them'.

We are obsessed by 'them'; the demands we make are for 'them', and not for ourselves. Whatever decisions are made by the French government, whatever actions are taken, it is 'they', the victims, who must be at the forefront of everyone's minds; everything we are doing is for the deportees, and what is left of their families, for those who have nothing, for 'them' and their poor wretched children, who may or may not be orphans. Our task in short is to provide a bridge between the world of ghosts, of the missing, and the real world.

15TH MAY 1945

'Not one death forgotten, not one tear shed in vain.'
Général de Gaulle 9th May 1945

And so it is all over. This evening, Europe is opening its windows onto the first night of peace, of light in the cities, the first without blue shades or black-out curtains or sirens, the first night on which no more young men will be killed, the first in which the guns, those monsters of war, will fall silent, their silhouettes raised uselessly to the stars.

It's over. Six years! Six years since that beautiful summer morning of 2nd September 1939, when tanned holiday-makers were still enjoying the beaches of France, beaches dotted with orange striped tents, where seagulls pecked about at low tide and children played half-naked on the shimmering sand, darting between pools left behind by the tide and made iridescent by the sun; while in every village people were gathering around the *Mairie* or in cafés, men and women

already in their separate groups, talking in low voices, and we heard the radio announcement: 'The general mobilisation of the army, navy and air force has been declared.'

On 3rd September Daladier[77] announced that we had declared war on Germany. A dark cloud overshadowed the world. It hung there for six years, enough time for a boy to grow into a man, for a man to reach middle-age or to grow old, enough time for those who went away to be unable to recognise their own children on their return. And enough time to see France itself become unrecognisable, and then to get used to the changes; time to lose one's entire family at a stroke, engulfed by this second war which was also a war against civilians, in which none were spared, not the elderly, not women, not children; time to see the crushing of the most insane pride, the defeat of the worst act of defiance against God in history, and to observe, with bated breath, as piece by piece, in storm and tumult, conquests were reversed – from Norway to Spain, Brittany to the Caucasus, conquests which had been more rapid and more widespread than those of Napoleon or Caesar.

It's over.

We're going to see the colours of peace again, breathe in its scents, the roses of peace; and when the leaves fall in the

77 Edouard Daladier (1884–1970) was Prime Minister of France at the start of WWII. He resigned as Prime Minister in March 1940, but remained in the government as Minister of Defence, until May 1940 when, with other members of the government he fled to Morocco. Arrested for treason by the Vichy government, he was imprisoned until 1943, then handed over to the Germans.

autumn they will be falling in peacetime. The sounds of peace will be in our ears. As children of the Great War we had been aware for twenty years that the sounds we heard every day were the sounds of peacetime: subconsciously, and almost constantly, we compared them to the wartime sounds of our early years. Now, once more, on clear summer mornings in the countryside, we'll hear the clack of the gardener's shears as he cuts the grass, the distant sound of trotting horses and cart-wheels on the road, the toot of a car horn, the spinning garden-sprinkler with its little hail of rain, and the postman's step on the gravel. In Paris we'll hear the wonderful, deafening roar of cars on the boulevards, impatient horns hooting along the length of the Faubourg Saint-Honoré at 5 o'clock in the evening, and we'll hear the traditional cries of Paris, in quiet, old, out-of-the-way streets, 'Rabbit skins! Skins!', and the rag and bone men calling out 'any ol' clothes?'; and we'll hear shouts of 'Lovely cherries, ladies, buy my sweet cherries', followed in the winter by cries of 'hot chestnuts, hot chestnuts . . .' around glowing braziers on street corners.

As adults we could still hear in our heads the wartime sounds that had been a part of our early childhood, we had never forgotten them; we recognised them immediately, harsh and terrible sounds that fill the air, deep booming noises that sent us scurrying down into the cellars, explosions that rattled the windows, or shattered them into splinters; noises that blot out everything else and give rise to an eerie silence, deadening the laughter of girls and of birdsong on a clear evening.

It's over. And this time it's ended in victory. Men and women are rising half-dead from their beds and getting back

to work; there's no time to rest when everything is in a state of collapse. Slowly the country is removing the dressings from its bloody limbs, cleaning the wounds and binding them up again, rebuilding and sowing fresh seeds. It's the night of the Armistice, and this evening I watched the people of Paris, of my city, doing exactly what they have done throughout their history on days of national importance – thronging down the boulevards, and assembling in front of the Arc de Triomphe, which shone like a beacon of light above the Allied flags billowing like the sails of the ship on the city's coat of arms.

So I have lived to see this night, to see this day, VE day, long promised by de Gaulle and Churchill, the day for which millions have hoped and prayed for so many years. I can remember every word of the radio broadcasts which, despite the interference, we listened to during the darkest days of Nazi occupation, and which kept us alive. I have lived to experience this joy. But it's a muted joy, and the cheers I hear are fitful: the young men are cheering, and so are the girls riding on the tops of lorries, waving flags; but the others, the older generation, the elderly who have chosen to stand in the streets, the sick who wanted to watch, these men and women are silent, they have tears in their eyes. In the midst of all the jubilation there is something solemn, almost sad even, in the flutter of the Freedom flag. That's how it seems to me. This is not unthinking joy, there's a bitterness in the celebrations: these people have suffered, for four years their country has been occupied, for four years they have been humiliated, treated like superior slaves, wearing a veneer of smiles and apparent contentment, a mask, which to our great

shame, all too many were happy to adopt, only to find themselves later hunted down, forced to buy off their captors, stripped of their possessions, tortured: but still they maintained the same false smiles, and in some cases the same satisfied expression.

These are the celebrations of a country beaten not through its own fault ('When gallant France was struck to death,' said Churchill in his speech to the French in December 1940), of people who, in order to conceal their rage and frustration, contrived to appear indifferent and resourceful, who faltered for a moment, then, little by little, refusing to be defeated, pulled themselves back up and, with daily increasing vigour, rejoined the fight alongside the Allies. Their forces were few and their resources limited but they did what they could, they sacrificed the best of their children, in spite of the occupiers' brutal reprisals; they worked underground and later openly, spilling at times the purest of their blood for the noblest of causes. These are the celebrations of people who have reclaimed their country, their own true country, who have proved themselves, once more, worthy of their forebears who fought and died in 1789 and 1792 and later in the Great War. But their joy is tinged with sadness, for these are people who have learnt what men are capable of doing, and they can never forget it.

I have quite clear memories of 11th November 1918. I remember the sea of people swelling the boulevards, to which I had been taken, holding tightly to the hand of a grown-up; I remember the shrieks of joy, the frenzied optimism, the innocent happiness, the kisses and the tears of an entire

population on the march. A sort of indescribable madness reigned: people were hugging one another, kissing strangers. For a few minutes we ceased to exist as individuals and became part of a great whole, our country temporarily overcome by a collective hypnosis that seemed at the time to be bigger than all of us, which carried us along so that we almost died of excitement there and then: without knowing it we had become one being, with a thousand heads, thousands of limbs, and only one soul.

I was a child, but the sensation of surrendering my identity to that of my country has remained with me always: 11th November 1918 marked the end of the 'war to end all wars', the end of dying for our young men and for our fathers, the end of the nightmare, the return to life. All the dead, whether they had died in the trenches, or in the raids, regardless of class, or race, or religion, had died, every one of them, for France.

It was the end of an epoch on 9th May 1945 and the beginning of an era, still shrouded in mystery and filled with hidden dangers. This has been both a soldiers' war and a civilians' war, and we have seen the doors open onto a world of which we knew nothing, a world of horrors, of medieval barbarism, and the doors are heavy and the hands of civilised people may not be able to close them again. It's a strange night, happiness alloyed by grief. We are walking in silence, choking back tears. There are ghosts at our sides: our dead friends are walking with us. There are the friends who died in 1940, in the battle of the Ardennes: I think of you, Pierre, always laughing; and those who were tortured, and shot, I

think of you, Albert, always top in everything, the cleverest of us all, shot in Toulouse, and you Michel, no one knows where you died, and you Jean-Pierre, killed in your tank. And there are those who died in the camps, I think of you, Georges, so charming, and ready to help everyone, without a thought for yourself, always giving us courage; and those who have not yet returned, especially you Emmanuel: I have tried so hard to find you, I keep hearing your voice everywhere, I see your smile, just as it was the last time I saw you. I'm thinking of all of you, of whom we have no news, who have disappeared, lost in the chaos, in the vast labour camp that was Europe. We picture you in a sort of limbo, somewhere between life and death, according to how hopeful we are feeling; we question the few returnees, who are straggling back, one by one, still in their blue-striped prison clothes, tirelessly showing them your photographs, 'And him? Do you recognise him? Have you seen him?'

'Not one death forgotten, not one tear shed in vain,' said Général de Gaulle. Must I say it? We French Jews are walking along on this most beautiful of evenings and sharing in the joy of France, but we have around us more ghosts than others do: not only our war dead, our Resistance workers shot in the Vercors and elsewhere, and the Jews who served in the Free French forces, but all the others, elderly parents, young brothers and sisters, those who did not have the time to do anything, nor the strength, who were torn away from their lives, from the country they thought of as theirs, loaded on to cattle trucks and unloaded at Auschwitz, where the SS, advised by their doctors, methodically despatched people to

their deaths, like Atropos[78] cutting the thread of life, with one simple barked order: 'Able-bodied to the left. Others to the right. Those unable to walk, in the lorries.' We know where the lorries went. And all the children went in the lorries, so many children, slaughtered because they were unable to work, thrown into the ovens with their mothers, who refused to leave them.

'No mourning, not one tear shed in vain.' Not even for those who will never come back, the ghosts, the innocent souls, who are beside us in the crowd this evening and who deserve justice? Our mourning and our tears are for our dead, whose deaths served no purpose, who did die in vain, who died for nothing, died like rabbits gassed in their burrows. When we talk of mourning and of tears, we are thinking, each of us, about a person we loved, or many, our families and our friends, every one a living, breathing human being, whose warmth we remember, whose last agonised glance we shall not forget, any more than we will forget the sound of their laughter, or the colour of their clothes, their pathetic luggage, or the last sight of them as they disappeared into the distance. These are the dead who could not die like soldiers, but were shovelled like bread into ovens. What was the point of those deaths? Is there a meaning to all that suffering? What am I to make of your words this evening, Général? Am I to understand that France is suffering the pain of the French Jews, which she cannot ignore since these are her people? These Jews are French, and love for the only country they have flows

78 The eldest of the Three Fates, she was known for her inflexibility.

through their veins; we know what anthem was on their lips when they left, and their patriotic cry when they died. But what about the pain of those who were not French, the Jews to whom France had given asylum, and who were arrested on her very soil, rounded up to order, on the pretext of 'checking their papers', then held for months in Vichy camps, before being handed over to the Germans? We know what happened to them next, to these *foreigners*, many of whom had given their sons for France. The wretched foreign prisoners of war are returning now to find no one, no wife, no children, all taken by our own French police, alas. Many people heard your words this evening, Général. Are we to understand that not one of those who have suffered will be disowned, however repellent, however alien? Can we believe that when you said 'Vive la France', you were including *all* the dead?

France, my country, the country where I was born, this evening you have made my suffering worthwhile. Paris, I should like to kiss the cobbles of your streets and the walls of your houses, and lie down on the ground, on my soil, in which I hope one day to be buried. You have embraced my ghosts, my dead, and those who are still missing, who walk alongside me, you have embraced them and they are with you again.

But what about the 'others', the distant cousins in the convoys and the camps, the ones who were not born here, and who were the first to suffer? What of their dead?

'Not one tear shed in vain . . .'

20TH SEPTEMBER
THOSE WHO SLEEP AT NIGHT

I am kept awake at night by the thought that somewhere in the world a man is hungry. . .

Charles Péguy *De Jean Coste*

There is a scene in Macbeth of unequalled pathos. Macduff,
Macbeth's erstwhile friend, has discovered his crime and
left Scotland to join loyal forces in England. There he learns
that to avenge this desertion Macbeth has ordered the murder
of Lady Macduff and her two children. Stunned, Macduff
repeats what he has heard:

Macduff: My children too?
Ross (his cousin): Wife, children, servants, all
That could be found.
Macduff : And I must be from thence!
My wife killed too?
Ross: I have said.
Malcolm: Be comforted.
Let us make medicine of our great revenge.
Macduff : He has no children.
All my pretty ones? Did you say all?
Oh hell-kite! All? What all my pretty chickens
And their dam,
At one fell swoop?
Ross Dispute it like a man
Macduff : I shall do so;

But I must also feel it as a man.
I cannot but remember such things were
That were most precious to me.
Did heaven look on
And would not take their part?

B had a wife and two sons. All three were arrested in the Isère in January 1944. They had been denounced by a member of the Milice. B waited for them, just like we all waited. Like us, he has stopped waiting. No doubt there is some part of him, some absurd and irrational part, which, in the silence of the night, still waits; in spite of himself, in a corner of his soul a particle of hope remains: though the hope is vain and the waiting futile, no doubt, in those long inner dialogues, he is saying, 'not both of them, not both. It's not possible. My little Jean will come back. He was always so cheerful. He must come back. Or maybe my wife and the little one, but not the older boy. The older one will come back. . .' These were big, strong boys, who were doing well at school, taking their exams when and where they could, under false names, and in spite of money problems, and the need to live in hiding in any number of towns in the Southern Zone: one of them even had a job on a farm. Months of anxiety, persecution and arrests, hard labour, cold and hunger – nothing changed their hand-some young faces. And yet they haven't come back. Madame B, exhausted by shopping and cooking, was gentle and modest. I will never forget her resigned smile: there was a courage about it to which, when I think of her now, her tragic end lends a sort of nobility. B continues to come and go,

146

puts on his tie and talks of politics, and no one knows what goes on in his head.

Madame P has been waiting for her daughter, her son-in-law and her three grandchildren, of whom the eldest was eleven: they were all seized because the father was too brave and too loyal to his post. Madame P is still waiting for them: deep down, she will wait for months, years. She is one of those women who would wait for centuries, for as long as human suffering endures, because however long and however senseless the waiting, a glimmer of hope remains. She will carry on waiting until she dies herself, waiting for her family to rise up again, in the flesh, all together, from the ashes, living, breathing, smiling. She is waiting for her daughter, a charming young woman I used to know, who was so happy, if all too briefly, with her husband, her children, her house. Madame P doesn't want to know about the station at Auschwitz, or the SS guards shouting their implacable orders, 'You to the right, you left', nor how mothers would lead their children to the gas chambers themselves in order that they might all die together, by the light of the burning ovens.

Per me si va nella citta dolente
Per me si va nel eterno dolore
Per me si va tra la perduta gente

Perhaps she hasn't read Dante? So what! What difference would it make? She will carry on quietly for years, imagining herself beside three little beds, watching three little curly heads, hearing three childish voices, and this will be the joy of

her old age, the reward for a life of dignity; when the weather is fine she will go down into the squares and watch other people's grandchildren playing hopscotch or catch and squealing with delight, under the eyes of their young mothers, who carelessly entrust them to the false sunshine of the free world.

André's father, an admirable man if ever there was one, was taken, together with his sick mother, and his aged grandmother, all denounced in the Isère in October 1943, and deported via Drancy in November. His brother was seized in a round-up in February. Not one of them has returned. He gave up waiting for them at the end of August. Perhaps he never really expected them to come back, but was just pretending to wait, fooling himself, making himself believe in order to carry on the daily routine of life and work. 'When my younger brother comes back,' he used to say. Then: 'If only my brother were to come back.' Now he says nothing. The time for self-deception has passed, and the rational man must look squarely at the pieces of his shattered life which remain in his hands.

I am reminded of Hélène B,[79] arrested along with her mother and father – this was a family that had been French for centuries. During the Occupation I used to see her cycling around the Latin Quarter, near the Sorbonne, with her books;

---

79 Hélène Berr (1921–1945): active in the *Union Générale des Juifs*, she was captured and deported with her parents to Auschwitz in 1944, before being transported to Bergen-Belsen, where she died in 1945. Her camp diary was released to her fiancé, who gave it to Berr's niece in 1994. It was published in France in 2008. Cf also. fn. 2.

the yellow star on her jacket was almost like a badge of honour awarded to this magnificent, hugely gifted young woman, whose thesis, though not yet finished, was already famous, a natural musician, whose generosity was admired by all who knew her. After struggling for a year with heroic courage, helping to keep her companions alive in the hell of Birkenau, she died one morning at Bergen-Belsen, exhausted, no longer able to stand, beaten to death by the woman in charge of the camp. 'She suffered more than Jesus Christ,' wrote her sister.

I must bring this list to an end. If I were to include just our friends, our family, and those known to us, it would fill a book, but I often think of S, a fragile creature who, having spent two years in prison for her Gaullist sympathies, returned to her two small children and waited for her husband who had been arrested during her absence. 'Now that you're here, Papa will come back,' said the four-year-old girl. Papa has not come back, and his young wife wrote in one of her letters to me, 'So, you see, I no longer hope to meet my E again on this earth. But I believe that if the blessed are in Heaven, E will be among them. "Blessed are the pure in heart for they shall see God." I cannot accept that I will never see him again, my own E, that I will never hear him laugh again, or see his tall young body, his way of appearing lost in thought, never see his piercing eyes, or his marvellous smile, which could light up a room. I cannot accept that nothing is known about him, that perhaps nothing will ever be known, not where he died, or how, or when, or by what appalling means; nor that we will never know if he was still composing poetry in the camp – he wrote such beautiful poetry – nor what dreams he had, what visions

he saw at the end, in his final agony, before, aged thirty-two, he died. For nothing.' I think that he and his wife will go on calling to each other at night, because those who love can hear from beyond the grave; they reach out to one another with arms of flesh and ghostly limbs, and at the moment when sleep seems close to death they touch and hold each other, close in a mystical embrace, which nothing can sever.

In the desolation that is Europe now, thousands upon thousands are searching for each other, calling out in the night for the ones they love. Thousands upon thousands have waited for each other in spite of the ever increasing certainty of the unimaginable horror of their fate, and maybe deep down we still believe they might walk through the door. Yet thousands and thousands have died, their suffering has been beyond measure, their cries can still be heard: they have no graves, they had no funerals, they left no bodies; they are calling for justice, to avenge their spilt blood.

The crime is without equal, the massacre was total. Only a handful have returned from the camps, all the rest perished: six million Jews in Europe, one million eight hundred thousand Jewish children, thousands of *résistants* of every nationality. We know everything now, or almost everything, about the extent and the horror and the nature of the German atrocities. The camps hold hardly any secrets for us now, and if each new account still makes us shudder, it is not from surprise, but from the dreadful excess of it. Our work will soon be done. Must we then do nothing but weep? Do we owe the survivors no more than a little help and a little love, and do we owe the dead only silence and oblivion?

'Dispute it like a man,' says Ross to Macduff, with his primitve, feudal notion of honour, and Macduff, with his own hands, cuts off Macbeth's head. On whose head could we take our revenge? It would take a Hydra, with a thousand heads, twenty thousand, thirty thousand, and we would never be able to cut off so many. And as for the survivors, those who remain of the multitudes of victims, beaten from dawn to dusk, of the martyrs, who, shamefully, were forced to fight one another for a crust of bread; have they got the strength, are they sufficiently attached to life, to dispute it like men, to seek retribution, to demand the justice due to citizens of a civilised world?

What are you complaining about? people will ask. The monsters of Bergen-Belsen are being brought to trial. They will be hanged.

Oh, yes. There is a trial taking place. All the correct procedures are being followed. English policemen are helping Irma Grese[80] out of the van, helping the woman who used an iron bar to beat the dying when they could no longer walk, and made lampshades from the skin of the dead. According to the newspapers she is wearing a light blue blouse and silk stockings, and Joseph Kramer[81] has said that the weather was fine. No doubt for a good number of people that will be enough, but for my part, I have to say, however much the trial reveals of the indescribable explosion of collective and institutional sadism that reached its apogee in Germany, in the

---

80 Nicknamed 'the Beast of Belsen', she was executed in December 1945.
81 Commandant of Bergen-Belsen, also executed in December 1945.

middle of the twentieth century, neither the trial nor the punishment of the 'Beasts of Belsen', as they are referred to in the *Daily Mail*, brings me any satisfaction. We hear that ordinary German people are shocked, that they are hurling insults at the monsters. How brave of them: faced with a mountain of corpses, isn't it about time fists were raised at the men and women currently in chains? But aren't all the German people responsible? These people with their gardens full of late-flowering roses, and their delightful daughters and their fondness for birds, are they not all responsible for what took place? They let it happen, didn't they, they let that poisonous climate develop on their own soil, and let it flourish over thirteen years, to become a breeding ground for injustice and blind brutality? In a country rife with fanaticism and idolatry, there must have been any number of twenty-two year-old Irma Greses. Everyone must bear responsibility for their own country, for their own political regime, and just as we in France are responsible for our collective negligence and our defeat in 1940, and for much of what followed, similarly every German must take responsibility for a regime in which Buchenwald had been known about for years. It's easy to appear indignant in the face of the crimes committed by these brutes, to exclaim that 'these people are monsters', and then go back home for a peaceful dinner and sleep with a clear conscience. For there to have been that many monsters, there must have been something unusually propitious for the gestation and growth of monsters, something complex which exists at some level in all of us, and in which each and every one played a part. Across the entire German nation Nazism produced a strange desire to destroy their world and, in a sort of collective intoxication, bordering on madness, to allow another to arise in its place, a world of death, a dark repugnant bloody and sadistic medieval world.

* * *

In France too, alas, things occurred that were both sad and troubling, in which a great many people were involved, some of them highly placed. And here too I have found that some consciences are easily appeased. Faced with the accounts of the deportees, the horrors of the camps, and the actions of the Gestapo, in certain circles people put their heads in their hands and heave a heart-rending sigh. 'Such horrors are beyond belief. These monsters deserve no pity, they must be executed.'

And how many formerly staunch collaborators, from the upper classes, captains of industry, appear genuinely shocked by the horrific actions of the SOL,[82] the Milice, the informers and the Gestapo in Corsica and in France? But perhaps there was more than one way of throwing victims to the lions, and these people too often forget that their firm allegiance to the Germans from 1940 onwards was deeply damaging to the country and poisoned the very air we breathed. There are after all people who don't take 8000 *francs* a month to become

---

82 SOL: *Service d'ordre légionnaire*, a far-right collaborationist militia created by Joseph Daraud, head of the *Légion française des combatants*, in the Southern Zone.

contract killers and steep their hands in the blood of others, or, like the professional informer in Nice, choose to hand over five children in exchange for 4,700 *francs* and two packets of cigarettes, or decide to sell their wife's favours to someone high up in the Gestapo, and get a further 20,000 *francs* a head for delivering up the local Resistance leaders. No, not everyone needs to sink that low. There are plenty of people who managed to hang on to their good name, and keep their hands clean, while negotiating a mere 800 million *francs* a year for themselves, in exchange for which, of course, they supplied quantities of tires, and trucks, and planes, and were the first to suggest to the Germans the idea of freezing Jewish bank accounts, or interning communists, while still maintaining their honour and their good name, thanks to their sky-blue uniforms. They say that a fish rots from the head down. Oh, yes, though there were some appalling men in the Milice – some, after all, were only sixteen years old – torturers, gangsters from Corsica, or Marseille, or Paris, and there were plenty of journalists who were guilty to a greater or lesser extent – words can kill as effectively as bullets, and the so-called articles that appeared in *Pilori*, in *Le Gerbe* or *Je suis partout*, were nothing less than incitements to murder and massacre; there was no end of propaganda, 'objective' reporting, like the article in *Paris-Midi* on Drancy and the daily routine of Jewish lawyers arrested in September 1941 ('6 a.m. Shower – we know how the Jews hate water – followed by manual labour for the community, and that will be the first time Jews have done anything for the community'); there were radio broadcasts, posters and books, and the messages they

sent out during the German Occupation were not just 'opinions' as people are saying now, but the lowest and most venal expressions of hatred. These miserable individuals at least had the courage to sign their articles, to follow through their beliefs, to accept the risk. But there was in addition, and this was far worse, an entire class of French society, a powerful, well-organised 'élite' who had accepted and arranged the defeat, who celebrated submission to the occupying power, collaboration and the reign of injustice.

Should we be expected already to have forgotten the dark years from 1940 to 1942, forgotten the appalling complicity, the insidious, almost smug cowardice, that shocking race for jobs, even by those who had no need of them, that frantic anxiety to please, to kow-tow, sometimes even taking a secret delight in doing so, like Molière's Tartuffe in his acts of false piety?

How cruelly betrayed some of us felt when we sensed the concentric circles of danger closing in on us and realised that our 'friends' would no longer help us.

I truly believe that if there are people who are able to sleep well at night, it can only be because they don't believe in ghosts, and because the ashes of the dead don't speak to them. I am thinking of those in the Unoccupied Zone who voluntarily handed over unfortunate foreigners to the Germans; and the civil servant in the Ministry of the Interior who, when asked by a member of a charitable organisation to spare the lives of the wretched inmates of the camps at Gurs and Rivesaltes, who were dying of cold and hunger, in our beautiful France, the first such victims, replied, 'I do not see the

155

need.' You, in your elegant suit and your carefully knotted tie, sitting behind your desk, and going to Mass every day, then considered so chic, where are you now? Do you sleep at night? I'm thinking of those who, in line with the terms of the Armistice, agreed to hand over all political enemies of the Reich to the Germans, whether they were Jewish or not: Breitscheid, the socialist leader, Theodor Wolff, [83] the famous editor of the *Berliner Tageblatt*, and many well-known Austrians. I am thinking too of those, doubtless the same people, who, in August 1942, handed over nine thousand foreign Jews from the Unoccupied Zone. And I am thinking of all the arrests that took place there in August 1942, then in September and October in Cannes, Nice, Toulouse, Marseilles, Limoges and Lyon, carried out alas by the French police, who were deployed in vast numbers to round up a few wretched old men, women and children, along with veterans of both wars, and send them to Drancy to be loaded into cattle trucks for deportation. We know about their journey now, how they were treated and what their final destination would be, innocent people, dispatched by our own civil servants because they were poor, because they were not born in France, because they were Jewish. It wouldn't be long before French Jews too were abandoned to the same sadistic monsters. There were

83 Theodor Wolff (1868–1943) was a founding member of the German Democratic Party and editor in chief of the newspaper *Berliner Tageblatt*. Increasingly unpopular with German nationalists for his reconciliatory attitude towards the French, he emigrated to the South of France in 1933. Handed over to the National Socialists in May 1943, he died six months later in the Berlin Jewish Hospital.

magistrates, who could easily have refused, who could have kept silent and retired with honour, as some others did, but who agreed instead to take on some quite bizarre duties as early as 1940, like sitting on, or even presiding over, the commission for denaturalisation and who now, four years on, are quite prepared to testify, at the trial of Marshal Pétain, to the fact that they did their best. There's one man who must have a clear conscience and a good appetite and no trouble sleeping and that's the one who went through the files with a fine toothcomb, selecting a mere 27,000 for denaturalisation (furriers, tailors, grocers, all now tidily at the bottom of their furnaces) barely three per cent of the total. He could have denaturalised many more: of the 27,000 names he selected to be rendered stateless and offered up, naked and defenceless, to the SS to be branded, then hounded by the dogs and whipped into vivisection laboratories, human pits, and filthy huts, only two or three turned out to be already dead, having fought in the first year of the war, errors on his part; several had lost limbs, and there were many elderly parents on his list who had been granted French nationality, only because they had sons of fighting age, and numerous grandchildren. . . Clearly he had much to congratulate himself about. It could have been far worse, and after all, if the war had been lost it would have been those people's fault. Marshal Pétain and the Justice Minister Joseph Barthélemy revoked the decree denaturalising one man whom I knew well who had died fighting in 1940, but his parents were not spared, and naturally they are long since dead, in the gas chambers of Upper Silesia.

Of course the president of the commission for denaturalisation could have done worse; he could have agreed to *all* the German demands, and signed far wider decrees. But he could also have done better: he could have turned down the job. There are certain crimes which should be left to criminals, and there were magistrates who were brave enough to say no, and threw their letters of resignation into the faces of their superiors.

Oh yes, all those zealous functionaries can sleep easily: after all they were only obeying orders, weren't they? Unfortunately many were high-ranking civil servants, *préfets,* the cowardly lords of our provinces, and I imagine the friends and supporters of the *Préfet* of Lyon also sleep easily, forgetting that the man they are defending brought disgrace on his position when he personally demanded that about a hundred Jewish children who had been hidden by Father Pierre Chaillet[84] should be handed over.

And doubtless Xavier Vallat's friends will have no trouble sleeping at night – 'he wasn't that bad' – and Darquier's friends, and du Paty de Clam's,[85] nor will their cousins and their nephews and their underlings at the Office for Jewish Affairs, tireless upholders of the law, official looters, and distinguished providers of cattle trains. The men from the Ministry of the Interior will be sleeping soundly too, the ones

84 Pierre Chaillet (1900–1972) was a Jesuit priest, theologian and active member of the Resistance. He evaded capture by the Gestapo, saving the lives of many Jewish children, helping them to escape into Switzerland and Spain.

85 Successive *commissaires généraux aux questions jaives.*

who took away the American visas of children who had already reached Marseille and had passports and affidavits to enable them to leave France, children who were already halfway to being saved, and having done that, took great care to look after them in order to be able to hand them over alive to the Germans. I trust that the same sound and healing sleep is being enjoyed by the brave police chiefs of the Permilleux section, who zealously encouraged their men to carry out the thorough searches of Jewish homes so as not to miss any terrified little children, and instructed them, when rounding up anyone living in hiding, to take a magnifying glass to poorly forged papers and to dispatch those whose physical appearance was suspect to the police station, first stop on the way to Drancy and Auschwitz.

I can't stop thinking of the words so often repeated, phrases that one would rather consign to oblivion but which still ring in our ears, every time we hear someone sigh, 'What about poor old so-and-so? After all, what did he do?' or, 'It's time we called a halt to this cleansing. Let's just punish the informers, release the rest and be done with it.' Of course they're absolutely right, let's draw a line under it all, let's not talk about it any more. But in that case let's hear no more, ever, from those men and women with their cut-glass voices who produced such outrageous statements: I am thinking in particular of the young Principal Private Secretary who, when I enquired about a decree making an entire family, one whose sons had fought for France, stateless and therefore liable to be sent to the camps, replied most solemnly, and with a certain resignation, 'What can we do, there are too many of them.'

Too many for what? Too many to be allowed to live? Let's hear no more from people like the appalling Welfare Officer who responded to a plea from one of the Little Sisters of the Poor for four kilos of potatoes and some noodles for a group of children hidden in a convent: 'These little Jews are a bit much, don't you think?' she said.

I ask you, members of the French middle class, my friends, my compatriots, why so many of you (not all, thank God: lots of you were wonderful, strong and brave) so often turned your backs on us, colluding openly or tacitly, without a cry or a gesture of protest, in a drama that was about to become a massacre. What did you think you were protecting? Was there something more precious than justice itself that you thought you could save by abandoning us? Because you didn't know, it's true, because you couldn't imagine the ovens and the rest, is that it? You thought it was all made up, propaganda, tall stories, even lies. That was because you lacked intuition, which is not the same as political intelligence: intuition comes from the heart.

The whole question of responsibility is impossible to resolve, I know. Everyone played a part, and retribution can alter nothing, but there is one thing we can hope for, which is that the failure of conscience that afflicted a section of French society be remedied forthwith, and that those people finally open their eyes and recognise what they did wrong.

Herds of innocent people were *actively* handed over to the enemy, but we cannot get away from the fact that there was also a tacit refusal to do anything to save human lives. Although it would not have been difficult, not one member of

the Council of State agreed to change the surnames which led
to so many being delivered into the hands of their executioners, in spite of many applications and much pleading;
visas were refused to all but millionaires, passports weren't
issued, Aryanisation was denied when it might have saved so
many spouses from deportation and death. Our papers, which
had to be regularly stamped, were checked repeatedly and
punctiliously so that we didn't have a moment's peace.
Exclusion from certain cities and compulsory residence orders
amounted to the perfect trap; 'statutes' designed to deprive
us of our status, of our property and effectively of our citizenship, were ratified by the most senior men, condemning
thousands of intellectuals and artists to a life of penury, and
ultimately to death when they could no longer afford a secure
hiding place. Worst of all was the deafening silence, which
started at the highest level and permeated the whole of
France, reaching as far as the welfare organisations at whose
doors we so frequently knocked in vain, the cautious silence
even of the Red Cross, whose ladies looked so pretty in their
uniforms, and so brave at the wheel of their lorries and inside
the prison camps, and who maintained their serenity even
when faced with our frantic appeals. It wasn't a malign silence,
and one could detect an almost cheerful optimism regarding
the fate of the deportees on the part of some of the Red Cross
officials, who appeared not to have noticed, in the course of
their polite inspections, the red glow of the crematoria, or the
stench of charred bones, the smell of Germany. The people
who were so bizarrely optimistic then, are the same ones who
have been pouring into France since January 1945 checking

on the fate of 'the poor German prisoners'. A worldwide conspiracy of silence surrounded a tragedy which was unknown
until then, and not one cry of protest was heard. If any of
those Public Servants and highly placed officials had been
worthy of their positions, if any of them had had any sense of
human solidarity, they could have kept some of the victims out
of the hands of the Occupiers, they could have provided cover
for them, they could have tried to snatch some back from the
enemy. Of course it would have been dangerous, but the
dignity and honour of mankind would have been upheld. So
many could have been saved and were not, and that is why *I*
cannot sleep at night.

* * *

5TH MAY 1946
CHILDHOOD LOST AND REGAINED

For the lost children of Israel, whose promise will never
be fulfilled.

And He said, Go forth, and stand upon the mount
before the Lord. And, behold, the Lord passed by, and
a great and strong wind rent the mountains, and broke
in pieces the rocks before the Lord; but the Lord was
not in the wind; and after the wind was an earthquake;
but the Lord was not in the earthquake;

And after the earthquake a fire; but the Lord was not
in the fire: and after the fire a still small voice.

Kings I, 19

Nothing leaves a deeper mark on a person's life than to have known war as a child. War violates a time that deserves to be protected, tranquil and safe, when the magic of dreams is untarnished, and where the sounds of the real world are transmuted by those who surround and care for us, so that we hear only a distant echo. We can all look back to our own childhood. Somewhere inside each one of us is a little playmate, sometimes laughing, sometimes grave, the witness and judge of our weaknesses, our follies, our desires as adults, a little being who has understood so much and remembers so many unknown faces, who is pure and shy and uncompromised, and who is none other than the child we were who will remain with us until we die.

The Children of War

Those of us who were very young during the First World War were still able to hang on to our childhood during those four years. The world was at war but outside the parts of the country that were actually invaded we could still live, more or less, as children. We had homes, we had our own bedrooms, we had our mothers, we went to school, we went on holidays: our lives carried on, even though our fathers were away. And yet the atmosphere of war pervaded all our lives, coloured our early years – France was full of sky-blue military uniforms and nurses in white veils. Our fathers were soldiers, their rare visits a cause for wild and excited anticipation: we wrote them clumsy little letters in big handwriting. Bad news arrived, communiqués were posted up at the *Mairie*, and words

steeped in mystery were etched forever in our memories: 'Foch, Verdun, the *Chemin des Dames,* Belgian refugees, matrons, Kitchener.' And then there was the mourning, long crêpe veils, all around us, pressing in on us, so that it seemed then as if women never wore anything else on their heads but black crêpe veils. Yes, we were children of the war, and even our games were war games. Even on holiday, the high point of our young lives, on those wide beaches where we spent long summer afternoons, the older children used to dig trenches: one group would be the 'attackers', another the 'wounded', and we, the little ones, were the stretcher-bearers. Sometimes the game was interrupted by the arrival of the telegraph boy, and one of the women would stand up, screaming like a wild animal, gather up her youngest child and run towards a distant bathing cabin where she would shut herself in and choke back her grief for her young husband. We are and always will be children of the war, the little children of trench warfare.

What can one say about the children of this war? The children of war grow up too quickly, like over-forced hothouse plants. The exodus, the long flight through France, houses, books and bedrooms abandoned, seemingly half the population on the road, with straggling bands of soldiers, and the defeat: that was enough to scar the lives of the children. But it was nothing compared with what was to come. Perhaps war, however horrible, is still within the bounds of normality. It was the Occupation that devastated everything. Wherever it was imposed in the course of those four years, our children's childhood was stolen, damaged beyond repair by the German Occupation.

There are no children in an occupied country, only young heroes, too young and too brave, or little old people quivering with fear, wild little partisans or little collaborators parroting their elders, intoxicated by a life of luxury and sumptuous tea parties, or urchins, barefoot and starving but proud, like the children of 1792 and of Valmy. They don't have time to be children. They have to queue outside the bakers', taking care not to lose the family coupons, and do the shopping for their mothers on the way home from school. At night they listen to the sound of enemy boots, and long for English bombs to fall. In the midst of defeat they long for victory; in the depths of humiliation their dreams are of triumph. They have to remember not to say the word 'Boche' but always to think it, to cut Vs in their métro tickets,[86] to draw crosses of Lorraine[87] inside public lavatories and on walls. It's exhausting: there is so much to do, there's no end to it. School is where they relax. In towns and in the countryside children are growing old before their time, becoming adults too soon and too fast. All over the world children of their age are looking for presents under the Christmas tree, while some of our children are helping their fathers hide quite different toys, shotguns and revolvers. Instead of enjoying holiday rambles together in the woods, our children have strange walking companions: they are leading English parachutists, or young Resistance workers

86 The cut corner symbolised victory.
87 The heraldic cross of the Dukes of Lorraine, consisting of one vertical and two horizontal bars, the Cross of Lorraine was adopted as the symbol of the Free French Forces of WWII.

along local tracks to new hiding places. When they run errands, it isn't always for their mothers; the letters they carry aren't for the post box: they are radio messages. Boys as young as thirteen-and-a-half are already members of networks; some fifteen-year-olds have already been sent to England, and even dropped several times by parachute in France; after the Liberation seventeen-year-olds received all kinds of medals, some even the *Légion d'Honneur*.

Yes, at the age when boys in parts of the world untouched by the war were playing football, ours were playing with grenades and machine guns, setting off laughing to games that could end in tragedy. Who will tell the stories of the children of the Ain, of Vercors, and south-west France, or the children of the Paris insurrection, whose young chests could be seen through their open-necked shirts, whose faces were black with gunpowder? Who will tell the stories of the young lads sent as look-outs; of all the children, French and Greek and Czech and Yugoslav, who wanted to play a part in saving their country?

Twentieth Century War was also a children's war.

SHAEF (Supreme Headquarters of Allied Expeditionary Forces) officers wore a triangular badge on their sleeves: the lower part was black, and on it was a sword which cut through a thin red line and pointed up towards a blue sky, the sword of Justice piercing the dark night of Nazism. For the children of Europe the night of Nazism was very dark indeed.

But for some children that night was twice as dark as for others, the shadows were twice as dense, and when each morning they were woken abruptly by the wan light of dawn,

their tiny hearts were pounding: these were the little Jewish children.

Everyone now knows what happened. Nobody wants to hear about it any more. They brush the subject aside, it's too unpleasant. 'There's no point,' they say, again and again, 'we know all about it.' Of course we know, we know how many children were sacrificed, we know about the war on children, the persecution, we know all about that. But what is knowledge? Knowledge is like love: the light of knowledge must be fuelled and kept burning, otherwise the facts will shrivel until they are no more than pale abstractions barely weighing on our too swiftly eased consciences. Like love, without passion knowledge is nothing. Knowing is not enough, not for us, not for others, and certainly not for those who have forgotten what they once knew. The time comes when it is necessary to break the silence that has gripped the whole world, and which begins to feel too much like indifference, or worse, like complicity.

They are still playing. . .

Some of us can still remember the calculated and insidious escalation that characterised the Jewish persecution: it is fixed not in our fallible and unreliable memories, but in our blood. The sensation of what it meant then to have children has never left us: they were in our thoughts every minute of every hour, day and night.

To begin with, of course, it wasn't too bad: parents always fuss, but it provides some distraction. There are things going

on. There are new games to play in the village where they have taken refuge, or in the surrounding countryside, games featuring a demarcation line, identity cards, the Kommandatur. In the Unoccupied Zone schoolchildren sing the songs of the day, '*Maréchal, nous voilà!*', or '*Une fleur au chapeau, à la bouche une chanson*', and the chorus '*C'est tout ce qu'il faut, à nous autres, bons garçons, pour aller au bout de la terre.*'

And they went, Marshal Pétain, some of your French boys, good children whom you abandoned to their fate, they went to the other end of the world, and you let them go: but they had no flowers, no hats, no song on their lips, and they didn't come back.

Returning from a history lesson, a little girl asks her mother if it's true that the 14th of July marks 'a black day' in the history of France.

There are training camps for young men wearing dark green jackets and jaunty berets, who cut wood, light fires and rewrite the verses of the *Marseillaise*, in a divided country full of sanctimonious hypocrites.

Little Jewish children in Paris are already bewildered by all the new regulations, by the ever increasing sense of being different and the posters that are beginning to appear on walls everywhere, and by the word JEW in big letters. The letters 'NO JEWS' are seared forever on those tender retinas.

The first arrests hit us like a bomb. In May 1941 the first 'foreign Jews' are interned at Pithiviers and Beaune-la-Rolande. The summer is fine, but overshadowed, and while our children go on playing, blissfully enjoying their holidays, we learn what is happening: in August '41 lawyers are arrested;

September '41 – round-up in the XIe arrondissement, the first round-up of Parisian Jews; December '41 – arrest of Jewish VIPs in Paris. That dreadful word Drancy, gateway to the unknown, is on all our lips.

Of course the children half overhear our whispered conversations and catch mysterious scraps of talk which don't make any sense to them – with good reason, for they are absurd. 'My family has been in the Vaucluse for eleven generations, I'm sorting through the documents.' 'Surely they'll do something for Pierre Masse.' 'The Chief Rabbi has written to Marshal Pétain.' 'We're French army veterans, we'll be all right.' And so on.

The younger children are as carefree as ever, but the older ones sense our changing moods and our forced gaiety; they know about our protracted visits to the *mairies* and police stations; they overhear us discussing vague plans for the future, possibly even leaving the country; they see our horror when we read the daily newspapers, our despair over German victories; above all they know that they must keep *silent*, silent at all costs. The other thing they notice is that we are not very busy, that their fathers are doing odd jobs around the house, and that the most important family activity takes place in the evening, once the curtains are drawn, the shutters closed and the doors locked, when everyone gathers round to hear the English broadcast.

The older children are well aware, and so to an extent are the little ones, of being different from 'other' children. Meanwhile we, the grown-ups, know that in the Vichy regime's camps, where the shameful malevolence of the state vies with

the criminal negligence of the local authorities, and with cowardice and silence, we French Jews know, from hearsay, that foreign Jews are dying every day at Gurs, at Rivesaltes and at other camps. We have heard that social workers are forbidden access to them, and that they are without food or blankets, that women are giving birth on old newspapers, that little children are dying every day because of the lack of basic hygiene. We know all that, but we carry on with our lives. . .

Then on 16th July 1942, the whole of France learns that, under orders from the Germans, the Milice have rounded up foreign Jewish women and children all over Paris – in Montmartre and Belleville, the Rue Oberkampf and the Rue Ornano, the Boulevard Bonne-Nouvelle and the Boulevard de Sebastopol. . . Fifteen thousand women and children have been hunted down by the police at nine o'clock in the morning, in the middle of Paris. Pursued right inside their homes, the poor mothers clung to the walls, wailing, overcome by an atavistic terror. Some even grabbed their children, kissed them and threw them out of the windows. While the Parisians watched, horrified, they were all rounded up, children separated from their mothers, and carted off in lorries to the Vél d'Hiv, and the neighbours had to keep their windows closed for three days and four nights, until they had all been taken away for deportation, so as not to hear the cries.

It goes without saying that the conspiracy of silence in official circles was total, and that the few Red Cross nurses who were authorised to go inside the Vélodrome d'hiver, were given clear instructions from above to say nothing about what they had seen. A few of these young women, appalled, did

later describe something of the nightmarish scenes they had witnessed.

Everyone knows what happened that day. Somewhere in his or her heart every Parisian has an image of that tragic day, of the bloody crime committed in the very streets where the citizens of Paris marched in 1789, 1791, and then again in 1830, and 1848, and in 1870 for the Commune, for Liberty, Equality and Fraternity for all, regardless of nationality or race.

After that we know that they will arrest and deport anyone who gets in their way, methodically, promptly and in an orderly fashion, French and foreigners alike, from veterans of both wars to the wives of prisoners of war and Polish seamstresses from the Rue du Sentier, and all the Jews like us who thought of themselves as French first and foremost, along with all the wretched refugees from Central Europe, of whom we had never taken sufficient notice. We know they will take anyone: men, women, ninety-year-olds, the blind, the sick on their stretchers, lunatics from their asylums; and if they need more, they go to the Rothschild Hospital and collect patients with gaping wounds directly from the operating theatres, and women who have just given birth, and who knew even as they were in labour that they would be deported with their babies before the week was out. We know that they will force everyone to walk, then kick them into lorries, hurling the children in like sacks, and pack them all off in death wagons to Upper Silesia.

What would happen to the children there? At the time we knew nothing. In our innocence, and because we needed to hope, we thought that the older ones might be employed on

the land, or maybe in factories, that perhaps they would be given jobs for which they had some special aptitude, that it would be very hard but that we would see them again. At the very least we would see the fittest and ablest: we would definitely see a good many of them again. We believed the elderly would be put in some sort of infirmary like at Drancy, and that the sick might be cared for.

But what about the little children? It's rumoured that they are being sent to farms, in Bohemia, Moravia and elsewhere: with no identity papers, or numbers, they could be lost forever. But we shall look for them, and we are determined we shall find them. It will take days, or weeks, or months, years even, but we shall find them. Where is the mother who would not recognise her own child?

The knock at the door

More and more people are arrested, in the Unoccupied Zone and in the Occupied Zone, everywhere, in Paris, Lyon, Nice, Marseille, Toulouse. Alas, the French police carry out those arrests on behalf of the Germans, following clear orders from them. Then, on 8th November 1942, the demarcation line [between the two Zones] is removed, and Nazi boots cover the length and breadth of France. They march into towns and villages, at night, singing. We hear them going by with all their equipment, we hear the guns rolling past, and their horses' hooves clattering on the cobbles until daybreak, and *résistants* and Jews toss and turn in their beds in the middle of the night, knowing what will happen in two or three weeks'

time once this army of young soldiers has marched on. Foreign and French Jews are already being taken from the countryside, from villages. On the Côte d'Azur people are being arrested in their hotels, and on the beach – men in shorts, children in swimming costumes, women in beach robes – and deported, with nothing, no bags, no clothes, sun-tanned and utterly confused, screaming and horror-struck. They are dragged, at a stroke, by the hand of Fate, from day into night, from the world they know, a world of blue sea and gentle waves and birdsong, into the unknown, into a world cold as ice and silent.

And the children? From now on they are nothing but recording machines, echo chambers, bundles of nerves stretched to their limits, taut and sensitive to the slightest thing. The poor Jewish children are just ears, hearing things which we are no longer able to keep from them, dreadful stories, terrifying snippets of information that are constantly being fed to us.

And we say, 'You're called Françoise Doucet, now, do you understand? Doucet!', and the children make us go over and over the names of our fictional relations – all part of our false identities – and even the little two and three year-olds know they have new names now. Little Jewish children listen and listen, they listen for every little noise outside, sounds which should be calm, redolent of peace, gentle rocking sounds, but which now might be enemy noise, a rustling of leaves, a mealtime ring at the door when no one is expected, which makes everyone stop eating as abruptly as if a spell had been cast, or the sound of a car pulling up at night outside the house,

the two doors slamming shut at the same time, followed by footsteps on the stairs. They listen for danger, and they watch, all ears and all eyes, but mouths tight closed, for our children keep silent, they speak only to us – sometimes not even to us – and in secret. And yet they manage to go on living a normal life of sorts. They go to school, when they can, they do their homework, they help us with the shopping, they do what all the other children do, they play cops and robbers in the street, they play marbles, the little girls play with their dolls, and ask for new dresses, and we put ribbons in their hair. Often they all shriek with laughter, then, suddenly, they are quiet, they start to listen again and watch. On the surface their lives are normal, but underneath they are living another life, constantly on the look-out for the unfamiliar, for danger, for anything that might be threatening, and their eyes are bigger than those of other children, their eyes open wider as they try to understand the secrets of a world which is hostile, incomprehensible and full of people who would hurt little children.

'Maman, there's a car stopped by the bridge.'

'Maman, the Gestapo are at the Hôtel de la Poste.'

'Maman, they say the man opposite is a member of the PPF.'[88]

'Maman there's a strange man walking up and down outside the house.'

'Maman, do you know what happened at the grocer's shop?'

---

88 The *Parti Populaire Française*: French fascist political party led by Jacques Doriot during WWII. PPF paramilitaries carried out beatings, torture and executions of Jews.

'Maman, Maman, Maman . . .'

Fear forced some children to grow old beyond their years. and their reactions to danger are quite remarkable. The children of the poet Pierre Créange, for example: they were stopped at the Demarcation Line with their parents, then came the usual scrutiny of their identity papers, the usual questioning. The Germans are about to arrest them all, when the oldest of the Créange children, in a completely natural voice, says, 'We've never met this man before, or this woman', 'We don't know these children,' confirm their parents. The two little ones keep up the pretence admirably and watch, without a word, as their parents are taken away, surrounded by German police. They will never see them again.

And I remember too the words of an eight-year-old, whose father had been arrested, and who had been picked up by the OSE[89] together with some other children. The little boy had come from Lyon to Clermont, and one day he announced confidently, 'It's very peaceful here, I'll arrange for Maman to join me.'

Young children, who lost all that was dearest to them when their parents were arrested, are the worst affected. A six-and-a-half-year-old boy was taking care of his three-year-old sister, like a mother, when they were found and taken to safety; he refused to eat any puddings, fruit or biscuits, saving them all for his little sister, whom he called 'my darling baby'. His sense

89 *Oeuvre de Secours aux Enfants*: French Jewish Organisation responsible for rescuing large numbers of Jewish children from the Nazis, setting up several Children's Homes for Jewish children of various ages, whose parents were either in Nazi concentration camps, or had been killed.

of responsibility and his love for her were so strong that when he was told that two excellent hiding places had been found for them, but that they would have to be separated, the little boy at first said nothing, then shook his head, saying, 'No. Never. Never. Never'. Tears rolled silently down his cheeks, and their rescuers recognised that his distress was comparable to that of a grown man. In spite of the risks, the children were kept together.

And they love. . .

But for children on the run, when their own parents were arrested, one of the worst problems, if one can call it that, was the transference of affection to substitute parents. Children form attachments very easily, and the hectic nature of their flights meant that one after another was broken. An abandoned child, who has lost his mother, after a day or two of stubborn silence will throw himself into the arms of the social worker who looks after him for a few days, then a little later into the arms of another woman, a concierge perhaps, in the Rue de Clichy or the Rue de Clignancourt or somewhere else when he's handed over to her in the middle of the night, silent and terrified; she takes care of him for another ten days or so. The child becomes attached to this simple, motherly soul, to the kind hands that make cakes for him out of whatever she can find, attached to her smile – and some do have wonderful smiles – and to her kind words. But then he has to move on again, to a fresh hiding place, and then a third and a fourth, and, in the dark night of a childhood on the run,

the faces to which he becomes attached begin to flash by like the lighted windows of a passing train. Time and again the child begins the painful process of attachment, and time and again, prompted by his anxiety, the same question forms on his lips, 'You won't leave me will you? You'll stay with me, won't you?' or 'I *can* stay here, can't I, with you?'

They played in the camps

Poor little Jewish children, who seem just like any others, you are desperate to love and be loved. Poor little children with your huge eyes, you were abandoned by the state, and let down by all the charitable organisations, but that didn't stop you singing, or enjoying simple things like a passing bird, or a cloud in the sky, because nothing is totally unremitting, not even the misery at the very heart of your existence. And what was so painful for us was seeing these children, who would soon officially be orphans, innocently romping about, playing and laughing in the sun, gleefully drinking in the fresh air, then suddenly stopping and saying, very seriously, 'When Maman comes back. . .'

Yes, they played wherever they were. They played in prison. They played in the camps.

They played at Drancy, in that sinister yard where countless desperate souls paced up and down, and who knows whether some of those hungry little hearts fastened on to the fleeting smile of some wretched internee, or an outstretched hand holding out a bar of chocolate; or if they spent whole mornings amusing themselves on the parched ground with a

blade of grass, or a sunbeam, with marbles or simply a dream. In the early days many little internees arrived together, ill, covered in scabs, without a drop of milk, or any soap, with no clothes, and only rotten straw mattresses to sleep on. Then they would be sent off in groups of a thousand, two thousand, three thousand, on the epic journey. Gradually, towards the beginning of '43, things became more ordered, hygiene was improved, and the small children who arrived on their own or with their mothers had a vaguely 'normal' life. Drancy was getting itself 'organised'. There were even schools of a sort, where mothers and social workers did their best to teach the children, using the books that we managed to send them, eventually and with considerable difficulty.

I have so much admiration for you, the mothers in prison. You knew what fate awaited you, but while you were waiting for the day of departure you went on washing your children's clothes, darning their socks, combing their hair, and stalwartly teaching them their lessons, as if they were going to grow up and become adults one day, as if the Germans were granting you a respite and were offering you the gift of life, your children's life. And until the final day, in Block 3, where you slept on the floor with your children for the last two nights, right up until that last icy dawn when the SS tore you from the camp and threw you into the lorries which would take you to the station at Bobigny, until the minute when you were forced to climb into the death wagon and confront the sobbing and the stench, and even throughout the journey, I am certain, you carried on chatting and smiling at your children to reassure them, and perhaps right up to the fatal

moment when you reached Auschwitz, where you hugged them tightly to you, while all around dogs were barking and men were shouting and lashing their whips, even in that hell-hole spot, so far from France, until the very moment you climbed into the truck that was to take you to the 'showers' you'd been promised, until the very end, Jewish mothers, mothers of all nationalities, French mothers, the ones I know best, who are so brave in adversity, as you went to your death with your children clinging to your sides, your babies in your arms, silent and terrified, desperate for the pathetic little pro-tection you could give them, looking up at you one last time to see your last smile, you never gave up hope did you? Deep in every truly civilised heart, in every truly human heart, there is a kind of mad intrepid hope, and you were hoping, weren't you, that they would live, that they would be allowed to live, that with your flesh and your blood you might be able to feed them, to rear them, to make men and women of them, worthy to be called human beings, unlike their executioners.

This evening, I am thinking of these children, the long lines of heads, dark and fair, all those chubby little toddlers, the rosy cheeked babies, and the older ones, the boy who said, 'I'd like to be a dog. They don't deport dogs', the adolescents who sang the *Marseillaise* as they left, calling 'see you soon', and the nine-year-old who asked his mother, when they arrived and were about to be separated, 'Maman, can I sleep with you tonight?'; remembering all the children who passed through Drancy in droves, between 1942 and 1944, and were sent by the SS to the ovens in batches – it was a remarkably streamlined operation. Tonight I also want to remember you,

their mothers, direct descendants of the sorrowing women of Egypt, Babylon and Nineveh who slit their children's throats rather than hand them over to the conquerors, grand-daughters and great-grand-daughters of the Jewish women of Alexandria, and Spain, and elsewhere, whose destiny it has been, time and again throughout the centuries, to suffer for their faith.

Unhappy mothers, my sisters, your tears still burn my cheeks at night. I pray that you have found rest and peace. The Massacre of the Innocents has been brought to completion: one million eight hundred thousand children have perished in Europe in the twentieth century. Are those dark blood-thirsty idols of the modern world satisfied by the Holocaust, the like of which has never been seen in the whole history of mankind, have they been appeased by the sacrifice of our children?

And I haven't forgotten you, Janusz Korczak,[90] a remote figure almost unknown in France, working in the Warsaw ghetto whose tragic history is known the world over. I am thinking of you, Janusz Korczak, doctor and poet, running your free school for children. You could have abandoned your little pupils and saved your own life, but you chose instead to go with them to Treblinka in the death wagon where the floor was covered in excrement and quicklime. And you went on singing to them, averting your noble head from those brutes, carrying the two youngest in your arms, like sacrificial lambs, held up before the madness of men, but offered to God.

91 Janusz Korczak (1878–1942) was a legendary writer, doctor and teacher. He ran an orphanage in the Warsaw Ghetto.

Moses is saved from the water

It's time now to think about the living, the children who are here now, the ones who escaped the massacre, like 'Moses saved from the water', the miracle children, these young Eliacins,[92] 'in scarlet robes', a handful of boys who came back from the camps, and tens of thousands of orphans.

For those of us who by some miracle, by chance, as a result of some error, or omission on the part of Fate are still alive, our first task, since the Liberation, has been to make life normal again for our own children, to provide them, if possible, with their own bedroom, their first for so many years, which they can fill with their own belongings, their books and pictures, and to impart to them all the knowledge and culture that we can give them: English and dancing, drawing and music; we organise tea parties for their birthdays, and sports if we are able. We are planning holidays for them, plotting paths for the future, paths of forgetfulness and of joy, and we keep a constant watch on their faces to check that there are no traces remaining of the past, checking that they are like other children. But what about the orphans? I must turn to the orphans. . .

The rescue of Jewish children is not complete. The youngest, of course, are the easiest to foster; everyone finds the little mites adorable when they see them playing in the children's homes, jostling each other, and shouting, dashing from game to game, running to lunch or tea; their eyes are

92 Eliacin was a Jewish king twice saved from death at the hands of Queen Athalie (in the play by Racine).

bright, their little curls, damp with sweat, stick to their smooth foreheads. I watched one lovely little girl, thinking herself alone on a path in the park, dancing till she dropped, in the shade of the tall trees, innocently sticking out her slender chest, and kicking up her slim legs in the cool evening air. This poem, one of several pinned up on the playroom wall, was written by a six-year-old boy:

> I got up very early
> I went into the woods
> I picked lily of the valley for Maman
> But Maman did not come.

They are still orphans. But it is the older ones who are the problem: the silent adolescents and the older girls, who are concentrating on their school work and will soon be looking for jobs, find the communal living hard and never talk about what happened. The boys are unsettled, aggressive one minute, apathetic the next, lacking the everyday support provided by their parents. Most difficult of all are the ones who escaped from Buchenwald, and who are still suffused with the trauma of the concentration camp: they present a raft of problems for those who are caring for them. For Jewish children the rescue operation is far from over. There are some admirable groups who are making a tremendous effort, doing what they can: they have opened a few pleasant hostels, and found people to keep the children clean and fed. What they achieve each day is a minor miracle, but it's not enough, never enough. What these children all need is to be taught how to live again, to

lead a normal life. A normal life. . . A normal French life which in spite of the horrors of war, and the enormous difficulties of the aftermath of war, is beginning to re-establish itself, after a fashion, before our eyes: the familiar sounds of Paris, which are music to the ears of Parisians, are returning. For so long Paris was a place of terror for its citizens, but in time it will become a city of joy and consolation again. But a normal life? Will that ever be possible, when so many faces are missing?

Can life ever be normal again for little Olga who, when she was nine years old, spent three weeks hiding in the family flat, abandoned there when everyone else was arrested, forgotten and living like an animal. Somehow she managed to survive, until the day the concierge found her by chance. She had tried to gas herself. Animals don't do that. We must rebuild a normal life for little René, the four-year-old who, when he was given some toys for his birthday, threw them all out of the window, saying, 'I don't need toys. I need my Mummy and Daddy.' We must make a life for the fourteen-year-old girl who, in the middle of dancing and laughing with friends, suddenly stopped and asked her teacher, bitterly, 'Why aren't we wearing mourning clothes? Why aren't we in mourning like the others since we've lost our parents?' We have to make a normal life for the fifteen-year-old boy who returned from Buchenwald a frail tottering skeleton and who, after a few weeks of square meals and fresh air, ran off one day like a mad thing into the woods; when someone finally caught up with him, he was in floods of tears, his face convulsed, and he screamed at them, 'What's the point of all this

food you're giving me, what good is this home to me, when I'll never, never ever see my mother again?'

Children are all the same

A normal life? My fear is that, while they appear to be leading a 'normal' life, the surviving children will all throw their toys out of the window. I am afraid that in spite of their wish to be part of the crowd, to forget and be forgotten, deep down they are never playing the same games. It's up to us to become a part of their lives, to share their adolescence, to channel their energy, tentatively to rebuild their shattered nerves. They are faltering on the threshold of their lives, and it's up to us to make them fit again, to support these dark, wounded souls, and to give light back to them. They were robbed of their childhoods and the first thing they need is the chance to be children again, however briefly. It's not a good thing to skip a stage in one's life, and growing up too quickly uses up all a child's strength at a stroke. These children have never experienced the magical universe of a happy childhood, never enjoyed the protective cocoon within which dreams can happen, or the deep, clear swirling lake that separates the child from the man. They have been denied the poetry which springs from even the most deprived childhood, so long as it has a firm foundation, one or two solid bases, a home, however modest, and a mother, any mother. All of this was taken from them: the power of dreams, of symbols that a child will nurture when left to himself, the secret delights of long years of childhood, the fairy tale quality that can embellish little

everyday things, even the most ordinary, the most mundane; the young child's magical capacity for story-telling, that ability to transform words themselves, words enjoyed for their sound, and not their meaning. Colette describes a child (perhaps it was Colette herself) who for a long time was enchanted by the word 'presbytery', believing it to mean all kinds of things, a butterfly, a snail, and who, one day, made the mistake of using it when speaking to her mother: 'Look, Maman,' she said, seeing a snail shimmering in the grass, 'Look at the pretty little presbyt . . .' The spell was broken. In every child there is a magic lantern that goes on turning as long as they have the time to be still and watch. Colette describes another child (she is such a fine poet of childhood, did she ever quite grow up?), a young invalid, bedridden, in whose imagination all the objects on the table beside him are wings to carry him away, even the ivory paper-knife, which turns into a sort of glider onto which he climbs each day to fly through the open window up into the clouds.

It is dangerous to make children grow up too early, to force them to confront the unremittingly harsh reality of life when they are not ready, when they are still too fragile, when it can kill their dreams and the love that is within them. When children have been deprived of their childhood, it's hard to give back even a little of it. If they are very young, it's still possible to get them to run about in the open air, to take them out into the woods in autumn, show them the excitement of waves at the seaside in summer, and there is no shortage of motherly souls, willing to try and give them something of the unique and unconditional love that they have lost. But can

anything be done for the older ones? They have been fatally wounded, flayed so that it's hard to know where to begin with them. At an age when what matters above all is to find themselves as individuals, they are forced to live communally, they have nothing which is theirs, not a single thing that belongs to them, not a piece of furniture, no memento to cling to in the anonymity of the hostel, perhaps just the corner of a faded photograph from their early days, without even a frame to put it in. What is to be done for them? What is to be done for these silent children with their blank faces, whose dreams are dead? They seem so unconcerned, so indifferent to everything, but behind that façade is a passionate desire to learn, typical of all adolescents. They are constantly searching for a book of their own, a look intended for them alone, the chance to take a walk by themselves, searching for a friend, above all a friend, more than anything they need a friend. Whatever the qualities of the people who are looking after them, however admirable, however caring, however clean and respectable the homes may be, these teenagers, sleeping six or seven to a room, have nothing of their own but a love that has been shattered, and the trauma of the past. They know now that the world is hard, implacable and fierce, and that if they are ever again to find the hope and the sunlit warmth of their early years it will be in the face of a friend.

We must restore their faith, we must help them believe in life, in other people, and, if possible, believe in their country, in the future of their country, and believe in themselves: all of these are linked. They must rebuild their shattered universe and recreate their myths, and, one day, each of them must tear

out the barbs which pierced their hearts and are still lodged within them. Because, in spite of appearances, they haven't forgotten their past, not in the way that little children do, naturally, unconsciously repressing events in their disjointed memories: for them forgetting is a daily act of will, something they have to work at. There is a reason for the silence, which we find so surprising in these children, who are at such a difficult age, on the threshold of youth, a reason behind the impenetrable silence concerning that part of their life, which was simply too tragic and which they have cast into oblivion in order to live like other children: the reason is that their past is too much for them to bear, because it can't be filed away, that they are somehow embarrassed by it, ashamed even. This is not true forgetting. It stems from a passionate desire to be like other people, at work, at play, in relationships. Occasionally they break this terrible silence, but almost only in their writing, which is full of violence and bitterness. Several of their poems and other writings have appeared in *Lendemain* – The Next Day – the title has a ring of hope about it – a magazine which is produced and printed by young people who have been helped by the OSE.[94] Some have been able to express their pain and their anger, in poems such as these:

A Dream

Sitting on a bench I remember
All that happened, all the pain
And this fine spring day

Gives me courage for our poor deportees . . .
I remember and then I sleep
I dream of a better world
One where no one dies for nothing any more.

and then there's this one.

Death's colours

My parents disappeared in green flames
I dreamt I heard the clinking of their bones
Burning and dancing
In the still blue sky,
Vile green assassin
With your red fire killing
My white-faced mother and my desperate father.
Vile green assassin, your soul is black.
Do not dare to hope for my forgiveness.

We must help them to forget their past, and to do so with a degree of serenity, to forget their past out of a love for life, an eagerness for the future, even by forgiving those who have hurt them so much. But before that can happen they have to acknowledge what happened, and stop repressing the tragedy, stop trying to hide it in some dark and shameful place deep inside themselves. They owe it to their parents to honour their memory, to transform the memory into something sacred; and above all to know and eventually to understand their history. More immediately they need to stop

thinking of their dead as martyrs, mutilated bodies, massacred and reduced to ash whose death must one day be avenged, and come to remember them as living people, wise people, whose hearts beat with warmth and love; they must think of them as they knew and loved them, and trust that they are now at rest with others in the peace of the kingdom of the dead.

It's up to us to fill these children's lives. It's up to us to help them understand the world they live in, to show them those things which are base and harsh, but also those things which are fine; they will meet cruel indifference but they will also meet with kindness and love; our job is to help them accept the human condition in its entirety. We owe them this support. It's not a gift, but restitution, not charity, but justice. In times of danger, people other than us, among the poorest in France, gave up their bread to feed them, gave them shelter under their roofs, and lent them their sheets to sleep in; they shared what they had put aside for themselves to help these children, who had neither mother nor father; some gave their lives to save them. Now that we have peace again, the least we who are left can do is to give up a little of our time and a little of our energy to help them grow up, to become part of the human family, to cease being creatures who are without friends, or love, or humanity, who are without hope. We must sow the seeds of a flourishing future for them. We must help them to make sense of their own destinies, to see that there is meaning behind the apparent absurdity of their tragedy; we must help them appreciate the dark grandeur of it, and understand that their parents died, like generations before them, because they

would not deny their race, the race to whom God declared to Isaiah, 'I shall give you for a light unto the nations.'

We will restore their hope, because they are our only hope in a world in which we have failed.

Persephone Books publishes the following titles:

No. 1   *William – an Englishman* (1919) by Cicely Hamilton
No. 2   *Mariana* (1940) by Monica Dickens
No. 3   *Someone at a Distance* (1953) by Dorothy Whipple
No. 4   *Fidelity* (1915) by Susan Glaspell
No. 5   *An Interrupted Life: the Diaries and Letters of Etty Hillesum 1941–43*
No. 6   *The Victorian Chaise-longue* (1953) by Marghanita Laski
No. 7   *The Home-Maker* (1924) by Dorothy Canfield Fisher
No. 8   *Good Evening, Mrs. Craven: the Wartime Stories of Mollie Panter-Downes 1939–44*
No. 9   *Few Eggs and No Oranges: the Diaries of Vere Hodgson 1940–45*
No. 10   *Good Things in England* (1932) by Florence White
No. 11   *Julian Grenfell* (1976) by Nicholas Mosley
No. 12   *It's Hard to be Hip over Thirty and Other Tragedies of Married Life* (1968) by Judith Viorst
No. 13   *Consequences* (1919) by EM Delafield
No. 14   *Farewell Leicester Square* (1941) by Betty Miller
No. 15   *Tell It to a Stranger: Stories from the 1940s* by Elizabeth Berridge
No. 16   *Saplings* (1945) by Noel Streatfeild
No. 17   *Marjory Fleming* (1946) by Oriel Malet
No. 18   *Every Eye* (1956) by Isobel English
No. 19   *They Knew Mr. Knight* (1934) by Dorothy Whipple
No. 20   *A Woman's Place: 1910–1975* by Ruth Adam
No. 21   *Miss Pettigrew Lives for a Day* (1938) by Winifred Watson
No. 22   *Consider the Years 1938–1946* by Virginia Graham
No. 23   *Reuben Sachs* (1888) by Amy Levy
No. 24   *Family Roundabout* (1948) by Richmal Crompton
No. 25   *The Montana Stories* (1921) by Katherine Mansfield
No. 26   *Brook Evans* (1928) by Susan Glaspell

No. 27   *The Children Who Lived in a Barn* (1938) by Eleanor Graham

No. 28   *Little Boy Lost* (1949) by Marghanita Laski

No. 29   *The Making of a Marchioness* (1901) by Frances Hodgson Burnett

No. 30   *Kitchen Essays* (1922) by Agnes Jekyll

No. 31   *A House in the Country* (1944) by Jocelyn Playfair

No. 32   *The Carlyles at Home* (1965) by Thea Holme

No. 33   *The Far Cry* (1949) by Emma Smith

No. 34   *Minnie's Room: the Peacetime Stories of Mollie Panter-Downes 1947–65*

No. 35   *Greenery Street* (1925) by Denis Mackail

No. 36   *Lettice Delmer* (1958) by Susan Miles

No. 37   *The Runaway* (1872) by Elizabeth Anna Hart

No. 38   *Cheerful Weather for the Wedding* (1932) by Julia Strachey

No. 39   *Manja* (1939) by Anna Gmeyner

No. 40   *The Priory* (1939) by Dorothy Whipple

No. 41   *Hostages to Fortune* (1933) by Elizabeth Cambridge

No. 42   *The Blank Wall* (1947) by Elisabeth Sanxay Holding

No. 43   *The Wise Virgins* (1914) by Leonard Woolf

No. 44   *Tea with Mr Rochester* (1949) by Frances Towers

No. 45   *Good Food on the Aga* (1933) by Ambrose Heath

No. 46   *Miss Ranskill Comes Home* (1946) by Barbara Euphan Todd

No. 47   *The New House* (1936) by Lettice Cooper

No. 48   *The Casino* (1948) by Margaret Bonham

No. 49   *Bricks and Mortar* (1932) by Helen Ashton

No. 50   *The World that was Ours* (1967) by Hilda Bernstein

No. 51   *Operation Heartbreak* (1950) by Duff Cooper

No. 52   *The Village* (1952) by Marghanita Laski

No. 53   *Lady Rose and Mrs Memmary* (1937) by Ruby Ferguson

No. 54   *They Can't Ration These* (1940) by Vicomte de Mauduit

No. 55   *Flush* (1933) by Virginia Woolf

No. 56 *They Were Sisters* (1943) by Dorothy Whipple

No. 57 *The Hopkins Manuscript* (1939) by RC Sherriff

No. 58 *Hetty Dorval* (1947) by Ethel Wilson

No. 59 *There Were No Windows* (1944) by Norah Hoult

No. 60 *Doreen* (1946) by Barbara Noble

No. 61 *A London Child of the 1870s* (1934) by Molly Hughes

No. 62 *How to Run your Home without Help* (1949) by Kay Smallshaw

No. 63 *Princes in the Land* (1938) by Joanna Cannan

No. 64 *The Woman Novelist and Other Stories* (1946) by Diana Gardner

No. 65 *Alas, Poor Lady* (1937) by Rachel Ferguson

No. 66 *Gardener's Nightcap* (1938) by Muriel Stuart

No. 67 *The Fortnight in September* (1931) by RC Sherriff

No. 68 *The Expendable Man* (1963) by Dorothy B Hughes

No. 69 *Journal of Katherine Mansfield* (1927)

No. 70 *Plats du Jour* (1957) by Patience Gray and Primrose Boyd

No. 71 *The Shuttle* (1907) by Frances Hodgson Burnett

No. 72 *House-Bound* (1942) by Winifred Peck

No. 73 *The Young Pretenders* (1895) by Edith Henrietta Fowler

No. 74 *The Closed Door and Other Stories* by Dorothy Whipple

No. 75 *On the Other Side: Letters to my Children from Germany 1940–46* by Mathilde Wolff-Mönckeberg

No. 76 *The Crowded Street* (1924) by Winifred Holtby

No. 77 *Daddy's Gone A-Hunting* (1958) by Penelope Mortimer

No. 78 *A Very Great Profession: The Woman's Novel 1914–39* (1983) by Nicola Beauman

No. 79 *Round about a Pound a Week* (1913) by Maud Pember Reeves

No. 80 *The Country Housewife's Book* (1934) by Lucy H Yates

No. 81 *Miss Buncle's Book* (1934) by DE Stevenson

No. 82 *Amours de Voyage* (1849) by Arthur Hugh Clough

No. 83 *Making Conversation* (1931) by Christine Longford

No. 84   *A New System of Domestic Cookery* (1806) by Mrs Rundell
No. 85   *High Wages* (1930) by Dorothy Whipple
No. 86   *To Bed with Grand Music* (1946) by 'Sarah Russell' (Marghanita Laski)
No. 87   *Dimanche and Other Stories* (1934–41) by Irène Némirovsky
No. 88   *Still Missing* (1981) by Beth Gutcheon
No. 89   *The Mystery of Mrs Blencarrow* (1890) by Mrs Oliphant
No. 90   *The Winds of Heaven* (1955) by Monica Dickens
No. 91   *Miss Buncle Married* (1936) by DE Stevenson
No. 92   *Midsummer Night in the Workhouse* (1962) by Diana Athill
No. 93   *The Sack of Bath* (1973) by Adam Fergusson
No. 94   *No Surrender* (1911) by Constance Maud
No. 95   *Greenbanks* (1932) by Dorothy Whipple
No. 96   *Dinners for Beginners* (1934) by Rachel and Margaret Ryan
No. 97   *Harriet* (1934) by Elizabeth Jenkins,
No. 98   *A Writer's Diary* (1953) by Virginia Woolf,
No. 99   *Patience* (1953) by John Coates
No. 100 *The Persephone Book of Short Stories*
No. 101 *Heat Lightning* (1932) by Helen Hull
No. 102 *The Exiles Return* (1958) by Elisabeth de Waal
No. 103 *The Squire* (1938) by Enid Bagnold
No. 104 *The Two Mrs Abbotts* (1943) by DE Stevenson
No. 105 *Diary of a Provincial Lady* (1930) by EM Delafield
No. 106 *Into the Whirlwind* (1967) by Eugenia Ginzburg
No. 107 *Wilfred and Eileen* (1976) by Jonathan Smith
No. 108 *The Happy Tree* (1926) by Rosalind Murray
No. 109 *The Country Life Cookery Book* (1937) by Ambrose Heath
No. 110 *Because of the Lockwoods* (1949) by Dorothy Whipple
No. 111 *London War Notes* (1939–45) by Mollie Panter-Downes
No. 112 *Vain Shadow* (1963) by Jane Hervey